NOTES FROM HAMPSTEAD

NOTES FROM HAMPSTEAD

THE WRITER'S NOTES: 1954–1971

ELIAS CANETTI

TRANSLATED FROM THE GERMAN BY

JOHN HARGRAVES

FARRAR, STRAUS AND GIROUX

NEW YORK

Farrar, Straus and Giroux
19 Union Square West, New York 10003

Copyright © 1994 by Elias Canetti, Zurich
Translation copyright © 1998 by John Hargraves
All rights reserved
Distributed in Canada by Douglas & McIntyre Ltd.
Printed in the United States of America

Designed by Peter Buchanan-Smith
First published in 1994 by Carl Hanser Verlag, Germany as *Nachträge
aus Hampstead*
First American edition, 1998

Library of Congress Cataloging-in-Publication Data
Canetti, Elias, 1905-
   [Nachträge aus Hampstead. English]
   Notes from Hampstead : the writer's notes, 1954-1971 / Elias
Canetti ; translated from the German by John Hargraves. — 1st
American ed.
       p.   cm.
   ISBN 0-374-22326-2 (alk. paper)
   I. Hargraves, John.   II. Title
PT2605.A58N3313 1998
838'.91203—dc21   97-26918

1954–1956

Slumbering in every human being lies an infinity of possibilities, which one must not arouse in vain. For it is terrible when the whole man resonates with echoes and echoes, none becoming a real voice.

I knew him back when he seemed to be made only of pretty little animals. Now grown like a weed, he has become a horse's tail.

He takes credit daily for having had a father.

Speak to yourself, speak—perhaps she will answer as you yourself.

He wavers uncertainly between his descendants and his forebears. Which are more reliable? Who offer him more?

Shallow religions: those we feel no fear behind.

To be sure, I *was* there; but sometimes when I read books about it, I manage to read myself away from there, and then I am quite desperate.

She is not stingy; she just can't stand people spending money on others.

Second meetings always ruin first impressions; should there be only first meetings?

He has settled himself in my territory but cannot stand the same sun shining through both our windows, so he burrows into the ground to hide.

"I have as little faith in concepts that are clear as I do in those that are unclear: either can lead one into darkness."

Johann Georg Hamann

To travel without dulling the edge of your sense of people.

The petrifying effect that F. seems to have on his surroundings speaks for the sincerity of his nature. He is in fact that which he thinks he is only pretending to be. Everything he touches—whether with his hands, his words, his breath, his gaze—turns to stone. He does not

(4)

need other people: he wants them to disappear. He does not even need posterity. For everything will revert to the stone he is made from.

He worships only this: hardness.

She wishes for a Jacob's ladder, so she can count her money in heaven.

The singers in the grave. "Thy son liveth, and hath the woman within, and they are singing. We went to look upon his grave, and we heard them; he hath the woman within, and they are singing."

Modern Greek

She is concerned with my loss because she is facing one as well. Through my loss she prepares for her own. She hopes that one day our two losses will find each other.

He studies and studies and can forget nothing: a dunce of dunces.

He has to keep on reaching: the "higher" things won't leave him alone.

Sometimes he gets quietly drunk on thoughts he has secretly stored away, and his happiness is doubled because he knows he has hidden them so well.

This aroma that surrounds people we don't know.

He explains all laughter as the laughter of derision.

Above all he yearns for the people he has found most unbearable.

The *rapidity* of intellect—everything else we say about intellect is just an attempt to hide its absence. We live for these moments of rapidity that spring like artesian wells in the deserts of lethargy; it is for their sake alone that we live, inert and barren.

"People say curious things about the dead and their wanderings. It's said, for example, that when one travels to faraway places—whether to Ife or Dahomey or Ewe Land—one meets them in the marketplace, people who died back home and have retreated here to avoid being recognized. If they see an acquaintance from home, they quickly slip away, making sure they are never seen again."
Leo Frobenius, On the Road to Atlantis (*from the Yoruba*)

Voice-sick.

He describes things in exclamations, he's that natural.

No sooner does the mere possibility of success appear on the horizon, than he tries to escape. His mistrust of success has become so great that he wants only to want it, not to have it.

There they can switch their feet, and oh! the different ways they're able to walk!

We can always find fault with the living whom we know well. But we are grateful to the dead for not prohibiting us our remembrance of them.

"It is noted as a special virtue of these people that they don't include 'tomorrow' when they count off the days."

In that country, everyone sees themselves when speaking to others, as if blind to all but their own images. Thus they are all very polite; they couldn't be more pleasant. Indeed, they are in a state of enthusiasm for everyone else, an enthusiasm only somewhat mitigated by their monotonous similarity. It is enchanting to see how they bow to everyone, when you know that they see themselves in everyone else.

"As she molded a clay pot, a Pueblo Indian woman imitated continuously the resonant sound of a well-fired vessel, to ensure that her work came out right and didn't crack in the kiln."

I should like to contain everything within myself yet stay quite simple. That is hard. For I don't want to lose this variety, much as I wish to be simple.

The mystic's nature is not mine; it seems to me the mystic sacrifices too much for his happiness.

I love to tell people who they really are. I am proud of my ability to instill in them a belief in themselves. I show them their own efforts. But I succeed only when I put myself into the effort. From my efforts their own take shape.

Today I got deep into Machiavelli. For the first time he really captivates me. I am reading him with coldness but little bitterness. It occurs to me that he studies power in the same way that I study crowds. He looks at his subject without preconceived notions; his ideas stem from his personal experience with the powerful and from his reading. One could say—mutatis mutandis—the same of me. Like everyone else of our time, I have experienced crowds of all sorts, and with my incessant reading I try to gain an idea of what the crowds of the distant past were like. I have to read much more than he; his past is the classical period, mainly Rome, while mine is everything we have the least bit of knowledge about. But I think we read in similar ways, at once distracted and concentrated, sensing and joining related phenomena from everywhere. Concerning crowds, I have lost my earlier prejudices; for me, the crowd is neither good nor bad but simply *is*, and our current blindness about crowds I find unbearable. I would have a purer relationship to Machiavelli if I were not also interested in power; here my path crosses his in a complicated and intimate way. For me, power still is evil absolute; I can deal with it only as such. Sometimes my hatred of it slumbers, as when I read Machiavelli; but my slumber is light, and I enjoy waking from it.

I didn't find the powerful figures I wrote about on the broad main road. The more I came across their names, the harder they were to approach. I am suspicious of fame based on acts in the distant past, and most of all I am suspicious of success. When the works of the great are texts, I can examine them the way anyone else does. But to what test can we put the acts of long ago? There is only the test of people's opinions about them, and these I don't ignore. But neither do I grant them honor or belief.

1957–1959

❦ It all depends on this: *with whom we confuse ourselves.*

How ordinary a person becomes when we see him often; it is as if he meant to avenge himself for the inflated image we have of him.

Changing one's beliefs according to the time of day.

For many people, the struggle to locate truth is like collecting beetles. Their beetles all look the same: gray and dubious.

Most men, he said, are slaves of an ancient misfortune unknown to them.

Somebody wants to get him to *define* things for money. But he won't even define things for free.

This tenderness toward everything we have seen before, and this revulsion toward so much we are seeing now.

Caesar makes me uncomfortable: the monstrousness of *action*. It assumes we have nothing against killing.

But do I experience *less* because I am just observing, or do I just experience *differently*? It's certainly not true that I shy away from people, that I avoid them. I actually get quite involved with people, but always only so I don't have to *kill* them. We may call this a priestly attitude. I find it humane. But we are deluded if we expect it from others. One must have the strength to see how they are. *My* cowardliness starts when I turn my eyes away. That is why I read till my eyes are sore, listen till my ears ring.

But can a person who doesn't kill ever accomplish anything? There is only one power stronger than the power of killing: reviving the dead. I am consumed with desire for this power. I would give anything for it, even my life. But I don't have this power, so I have nothing.

Even Caesar, who *pardoned* so many men, knew this power. How angry Cato's suicide made him!

Today I detected a downright murderous lust in myself as I was reading Plutarch's *Caesar*. When the conspirators went after him with their daggers, as one after the other stabbed him again and again, as he tried to escape their blows "like a wild beast," I experienced a sense of joyous arousal. I felt not a hint of pity for him. The unsuspectingness of this horribly intelligent "beast" did not move me to feel for him. His blindness was, in a way, a kind of retribution for all those whom he had blinded and trapped.

"Great": he who escapes seemingly imminent death often enough. How he brings about this danger in the first place is his affair.

His fear of all his endless little notebooks! By now they are mounting into the hundreds, every page covered, and he never opens a one of them! This prolific writer of nothing, what is so important for him to tell no one?

Anything to do with *order* is best learned from the Chinese.

I haven't read enough magic spells. Last night I was captivated by the Atharvaveda, the Indian book of magic. Uncanny things in that book—nowhere are human wishes expressed more *openly*. It is a completely elementary world, and if we really want to learn about humankind, then we should look not only at myths but also at spells, which are *naked*.

Love for the forgotten gods, as if some kind of inner greatness had caused them to retreat.

I admire those very broad people who through the decades become broader and broader yet *do not give in*. But the unyieldingly narrow are horrible.

A sucker for cemeteries—anywhere else, he's afraid.

A world without *gifts*.

I think it is the nearness of *myths* that has caused this uneasiness in me. I am drowning in them; all their power is turned against me. What an undertaking, to want to know them all—me, a small, solitary man of fifty, a nothing!

I am fascinated by the ancestor stones of the Aranda.

The naked old men crouch on the ground around the stones, the *churingas*. They gaze at them solemnly, picking some of them up in their hands and weeping.

How poor I am compared with an old Aranda! All the myths and traditions are constantly with him, in all their clarity, and for him, what they say is what they mean. Compare that with our noncommittal sciences, their feeble attempts at "interpretation," their endless vacuous analogies. When does one finally know what is important, what is immutable? No matter where one turns in our world, it is all equally huge, equally tiny; everything is equally distorted and out of proportion.

The Arandas of old are all dead. Now they exist only in books. These books are my *churingas*, my ancestor stones.

What I find most repulsive about people are their *plans*.

As they do anywhere else, people here live under pressure, but they don't yell about it, they just exchange pleasantries.

But what is the use of this sterile life of *proofs*, when we know everything beforehand anyway?

There is something sickening about all advocacy: only pure admiration is real.

I cannot even say how indifferent I am to the question of whether I will *prevail*. I want to find what I sense is there, that's all.

It is important to say all the great thoughts again, without knowing that they have already been said.

Whoever knows the truth about someone destroys that person, unless he keeps quiet. But it is hard to be silent around those we see often. We have to say things to them that help them without changing them. They receive so much help that they form a false self-image, and for this image we must take responsibility. At every moment we see just how false, and it is precisely this insight from which we must constantly protect them. No matter that we have protected them from themselves so long; they need this protection indefinitely. So we must lie, and this kind of lying is what makes life unbearable: continuing to spin false, bad fiction.

She walks as if she were being allowed to for the first time.

Now that I have thrown myself completely into my "field" and am getting deeper and deeper into it, I sometimes ask myself: am I, too, a specialist? And how much have I set aside permanently, never to be interested in again? Or can someone whose passions are religion and mythology in fact never be a specialist? Do not myths include *everything*, as I often like to tell myself, or is there something that exists beyond all myths? Is there a new myth, completely unheard of, and is it my purpose in life to search for it? Or will I end up a pitiful wretch, with a mere inventory of all myths?

I don't want to know the answer to this question.

The heat of eight suns: "In the mists of prehistory the sun had seven sons, which each burned down upon the earth just as hotly as the sun itself."

from the Batak

Is it characteristic of "the beautiful" that it can never be seen again? Our perception of it is at once sudden and serene: we want to see it as a whole, without interruption, *forever*. Seen again, it is never the same—unless we failed to see it whole the first time.

Wholly perceived, beauty continues to exist only within ourselves—it has lost its connection to reality. While we are taking it in, the image becomes tangible, as if we had carefully picked it up, and only thus can we receive it entire. This does not occur through suddenness alone, no matter how sudden it may have seemed.

It probably has to *begin* suddenly, but without that subsequent moment of calm, it dissipates and disappears. For something to appear beautiful it must be permeated by both suddenness and serenity: the flash of the eye and the quiet patience of the hands.

If we surround ourselves with "beauty," we live in a grave of beauty. Painful to think of Pharaoh's soul, oblivious to all those objects placed around him: practical, supposedly, but not beautiful, not to him—but surely to the one who opens the grave.

A snail that can call and a snail that can jump:

"The large Achatina Marginata, for instance, possesses the power of screaming. This fact is well known to the natives, who were much amused at my start of surprise when one of these Snails screamed on being taken into my hand. It is supposed that the noise is produced by the creature scraping against its shell. Anyhow, the sound is loud enough to prove distinctly startling on a first experience.

"Another small land snail has the power of springing three to four feet."

P. A. Talbot, In the Shadow of the Bush

He who would know all will lose his way in the expanding realm of his own ignorance. Every new insight I have won has come to me out of the unmediated observation of a single concrete phenomenon, not through analogy, not by assembling masses of documents about one and the same phenomenon. No one thinks in statistics; for the profound questions, all statistical methods are worthless. I must have the courage to continue to *select* that which seems important or meaningful to me. I must risk being decried as ignorant by every expert, in every speciality. This vain desire to know everything, which has pursued me since childhood, is something I must get over.

My library, which consists of thousands of books I have undertaken to read, is growing ten times faster than I can read. I have tried to expand it into a kind of universe where I can find everything. But this universe is growing at a dizzying pace. This pace will never slacken; I feel its growth physically within me. Every new book I add sets off a mini-catastrophe that only subsides when the book is seemingly brought into line on the shelf and temporarily disappears.

"If one is a *djama* (a prophet in Malinka society) one no longer knows the difference between what has been and what will be."

Definition of the Prophetic

The scars of zealots are still visible on his spirit.

We often say things to ourselves to forget them. But sometimes we say them too well.

Someone who doesn't know he is breathing.

He loves her; he can't be as careful with anybody else.

Sometimes in this dreadful wasteland a name is heard, and every grain of sand blossoms.

Why are you always explaining everything? Why do you always want to find out what's *behind* things—behind *this*? behind *that*? How about a life on the surface? Would that be happy? And would that be a reason to despise it? Maybe there is much more to a surface—maybe everything not on the surface is false, maybe you are just living in an ever-changing series of delusions, not beautiful like those of gods but empty like those of philosophers.

Perhaps it would be better for you to just arrange words one after another (since it has to be words), but you're always looking for a *meaning*, as if what you invent could give the world a sense it does not have.

He collects his writers like butterflies, and under his care they turn into one great caterpillar.

The man who was so good he forgot his name.

The fearful angel of the eye: "Too much—you have seen too much." No, much too little.

"One heart told me this, one heart told me that."
Rwandan saying

We forget nothing, and we forget it less and less.

You want someone with whom to discuss everything *afresh*, everything that you have loved; you want to sing the praises of it all again. To praise is wonderful, irresistible. Happy the singer of the Psalms.

Why do we suddenly have to have that which we really don't want at all? As if we had to acquire the habit of wanting everything.

Stories of people who do everything to stop being themselves. They transform themselves into their enemies.

Speeches, crazy speeches, and it all comes true. The prescience of words.

It is true that I wish to learn everything that men have believed in. But I want to experience it as it was when it deserved belief, and not in its exhausted form.

The conceptual holds so little interest for me that even at fifty-four I have actually never read either Aristotle or

Hegel. It is not just that I don't care about them; I *distrust* them. I cannot accept that the world was conceivable for them even before it was really known. The stricter, the more systematic their thinking, the greater the distortions they brought to the world. I want truly to see and think in a new way. That is not so much out of arrogance, though it might seem so, as out of an inextinguishable passion for humankind and a growing belief in its inexhaustibility.

Sahagun: a name of questionable wisdom.

The priceless sayings of fools, so long as they're not repeated.

"Without the perfect law of freedom, man would be incapable of imitation, on which all education and received knowledge are surely based: for of all creatures, man is the greatest mimic."

Johann Georg Hamann

You think you have everything, she thinks she has nothing. You live together. How *do* you live?

It is apparent that the object of hatred does change, but not too quickly or too often. Hatred needs time to attract things; this is not hard to comprehend. But how do these astonishing shifts in hatred arise? Why this one today, and that one next year? Undeniably, it is easiest to hate the people one knows well. We remove them from the fabric of habit, we isolate them. Their menacing quality is our own creation. It's unimportant whether they are dangerous or not. We lend them our old, unforgotten fears. And on these they feed—but all of a sudden we release them. We should understand this moment: when and why do we let them go? Have we recognized their menace as our own? Have we unveiled them and discovered ourselves underneath?

But before this can happen, we make them perform a curious dance.

1960

꙲ Slowly he lifts the heavy stones, a little higher with every sentence, and there is nothing that can redeem him except *his own words*.

The deceitful quality of noise.

My god: all eyes, and all closed.

All that he does not know might be beautiful. What he does know is covered with dark lava.

How do I feel about my finished book? It reads well, better and better, perhaps. I am not unhappy with it. What alarms and depresses me is the time I spent on it. If it had been one book among five or six, how proud I could be of it! For half a lifetime it is too little.

I think of the magnificent *Chartreuse*—a hundred years from now will I make even one person happy?

I think there is no one I love as much as Stendhal. He is the one, the only one, I envy. Perhaps I could be like him if I were not myself. This is the first time I have considered the idea of a different birth, and this only out of love for Stendhal.

What does this really mean? It means that I want to get out of the skin of my work, that I have carried my thoughts within me too long and now they have become my bones. In this sense, I am a *churinga*, or a stone in the Australian landscape. But I am still alive, and now my most ardent wish is *to be transformed*.

To become incomprehensible even to you, to stammer.

In my new existence I should like to be more caring but, at the same time, less ruled by compassion. As has become increasingly clear in the past years, the odd constitution of my nature has often led to a wasteful expenditure of energy without results. Filled with enthusiasm for the particularity of every individual who came my way, I have gone to great lengths to peel away the layers of their nothingness, to isolate and extract the unique quality of each. I have been so serious about this that people have become my "slaves." But their helplessness has made me feel sorry for them, and instead of being hard on them for their own good, I have given in to them more and more, finally letting them consume me. It began with the pure glowing image that I formed of them and ended with their first presuming on me, then consuming me.

My obstinate rejection of time is now taking its revenge on me. Its passing never existed for me. I never felt it as a river that could dry up. It was all around me, inexhaustible, a sea. I drifted about in all directions; it seemed natural to go on this way. My time would never run out. Everything I undertook was for eternity, and eternities were at my disposal, even for the smallest projects.

I was in search of the old gods, wanted to reconcile them within myself. My intellectual ambitions were fulfilled in the study of many peoples: this was how I atoned for the arrogance of my own forebears. I did not look to history for guidance. The smallest things, because they were on the verge of disappearing, meant more than the biggest. I could not accept ignoring a single life. Whatever this crowded world had no room for, I made a place for within myself. And so now I feel as broad as the world: I feel I touch it everywhere. Year by year the arrogance of those who live for themselves alone seems more and more alien to me. Today I know how little I am myself, how much of me is in the universal breath of the spirit.

But having attained this goal, I recognize my own futility. I have scorned time, and now it is running out on me.

The things one depends on in the course of a life are grotesque, and it is hard to see how one can guard against them without models.

Telling stories to anyone who will hear them as stories, who doesn't know you, who doesn't expect literature. Life as a wandering storyteller would be nice. Someone says the word, and you tell the story. You never stop, day or night, you go blind, you lose the use of your limbs.

(29)

But your mouth still serves its function, and you speak whatever is in your head. You have no possessions, only an infinite, ever-growing number of stories.

Nicest of all would be if you could live on words alone and did not even need to eat.

Cover any traces of the work.

Pavese was my exact contemporary. But he started working earlier and took his life ten years ago. His journal is a kind of twin to mine. He cared mostly about literature, unlike me. But I happened onto myths and ethnology earlier. On December 3, 1949, eight months before his death, he wrote the following in his journal:

"I have to find:

W.H.I. Bleek and L. C. Lloyd, *Specimens of Bushman Folklore*, London, 1911."

This book has been in my possession for sixteen years, since 1944. I have often considered it the most important book I know. The sheer quantity of new information about the unknown makes it my most important book: I have learned the most from it, and it is still not exhausted. This book, which Pavese turned to just before his death, is what we have most in common, and I wish I could give it to him.

On March 14, 1947, there is this sentence: "Hemingway is the Stendhal of our time."

I find this appalling and outrageous. Perhaps there is something to it, but I am too upset about the statement to judge. I am horrified that anyone could make it. It is as if someone wanted to dispel the mystery of Stendhal, the source of his greatness, with a cheap and obvious Americanism. Pavese was an admirer of Americanism; I am not. Thus Pavese could be called a modern writer; I could not. I am a Spaniard, an old Spaniard of today . . .

It is very odd that I feel such a kinship with Pavese, of whom I know nothing outside his journals. I feel so related to him that such an unexpected utterance angers me profoundly.

I am under the impression that he destroyed himself for an American woman.

"26 April. Wednesday. Certainly in her is contained not only herself but *my* entire past life, an unconscious preparing—America. . . ."

Strictly speaking, I have actually *hidden* myself from America up till the present. Its only real influence on me has been *Poe*, whom I read very early, perhaps at twenty. In this respect I am not different from many nineteenth-century writers. Hemingway rolled off me like water.

From 1942 to 1950 Pavese's journals run parallel with my own. Never before have I been so astonished by such parallelism. But I must assemble my earlier, sparer writings and bring them into some kind of order. Even prior to 1942 I was not mute, just less resolute.

You should read your contemporaries as well. You can't get nourishment from roots alone.

You spoke about it to everyone so much and for so long, with nothing to show for it—there never was anything to see. Then people just believed you. Now they have it in hand, a book: what is the use of their believing something now?

How do you forget a work like that? How do you erase the traces? It is like a horrible deed. You can't get it out of your head. For a while you can hide everything associated with it. But you are totally covered with it, as if it were vermin. Inside, outside, everywhere the same pestilence.

Perhaps you should invent yourself a new biography. Still you, but everything different from the way it was. Other places, other origins. Make up the most improbable tales for your own life story. Look for anything that wasn't the way it was. Thus you evade the hundred different paths that led you into the work. Were you, say, born in another time? Or will a completely different place suffice?

I need new *churingas*. New ancestors. New destinies. *New memories.*

You need an army of *termites* that will undermine all your ties and habits from within.

I must find my way back to my bushmen as an innocent, as if I had used nothing from them for the book. After all, what I used was only for those few pages about premonitions. All the rest is still "immaculate."

I am happy about my new brother, Pavese. But this should not occur often. We only learn from those who are quite different from us. With relatives, we are complacent.

Pavese's journals: all the things that preoccupy me, crystallized in another way. What luck! What a liberation!

His death prepared for: but nothing is abused, no emotion for him aroused. It just comes as if it were natural. But no death is natural. He keeps his death to himself, private. We hear about it, but it sets no example. No one would kill himself because he did.

And yet last night, when in my deepest depression I wanted to die, I reached for his journals, *and he died for me.* Hard to believe: through his death, today I am reborn. This mysterious process should be looked into, but not by me. I will not touch it. I want to keep it secret.

The blind man as traveler.

Barking men: it's a matter of marrow.

A ceremonial beast, assembled from tiaras.

A man who has yet to see himself.

Becoming as incomprehensible as the babble of angels.

Pentecost 1960. As warm as summer, a southern day, a Sunday of slow people in the heat. I read here and there, in this language and that: the day before yesterday Democritus, yesterday Juvenal, today Montaigne; a few days ago poems of Tasso. There is neither tension nor anger in me. I speak to whoever calls. Since the book appeared, total silence has reigned. At first I was puzzled, maybe a little bothered, but now the silence has entered me and I am happy. I am not tempted to go anywhere. I don't know what to do next. I am waiting, waiting for the thunderbolt and the powerful voice. I am still not free from all I have written up to now. What's past does not appeal to me, and I see no new goal. I often regret that my mind never acquired an English wardrobe. I have been here now for twenty-two years. Certainly I have listened to many people speaking to me in the language of this country, but I have never listened to them as a writer, I have merely understood them. My own anguish, my wonderment, and my exuberance have never made use of their words. Whatever I have felt or thought or had to say has presented itself to me in German words. Asked why this has been so, I have had persuasive explanations: the most important reason, and the one in which I have believed myself, has been pride.

Today I am tempted to begin life in a new language. I love this place I live in more than anywhere else; it is as familiar to me as if I were a native. Ever an alien, I have found a home here: the split between this homeland and my internal monologue is complete.

I would really like to loosen up. Everything in me is too tightly wound; I am always aware of a direction, a goal.

Nothing around me breathes. I have a world of my own, but how narrow it is! It is stifling me: what kind of world is that? I must let myself be borne along by my own invention again, without knowing where it will take me.

To *dismantle* noise.

Find a man who fears no one because he has never known anyone well enough.

Painting the cheap cloak of happiness.

The *grateful*—a burlesque.

I cannot help myself. In the greatest misfortune I, the unbeliever, await miracles. Of all the old doctrines of faith, only one has remained intact for me: the miracle. But I don't want to know where it comes from; I don't want to make one happen. It should remain just what it is, inexplicable, intractable, just a miracle.

The miracle as the all-encompassing, supreme transformation.

He never lived so intensely as when under the burden of direst defeat.

The idea of a human being without hope is unthinkable. What is hope? Hope is the knowledge of continuing cycles of respiration, as long as they are not numbered.

The hardest thing is to stop learning. It amazes him that a student can die.

Your early difficult relationship with God was nothing but an attempt to wrest power from him.

I breathe free only over blank paper. My atman, my soul, is in paper.

Stendhal has become so important to me that I have to turn back to him every five or six months. It does not matter at all which work it is, so long as the sentences contain the breath of his spirit. Sometimes I'll read twenty or thirty pages of Stendhal and think I will live forever. I have countless projects of my own before me, and then with incredulous horror I tell myself that he died at fifty-nine.

Stendhal's head was filled with things of "culture"— pictures, books, music—many of which are as important to me today as they were to him then. Many more are indifferent or repellently "sentimental"; the important point is *how* he was taken up by these things. He extracts from everything only that which is like himself. Thus I can perhaps console myself for being so preoccupied with barbarians and religions, since it is possible that they have become very much like me. Whether it's Canova or Wotruba, the accident of birth plays only an external role here. The passion with which one possesses every object and the passion with which one distances oneself in contemplation of it—that is everything.

Only the skeptic can really gauge the joy of belief.

The sole splendor of your language is the names of all the bygone gods.

Vanished thoughts that are felt but never found again.

All that delights him passes like a cloud over the earth.

With the passing years, even Despair eats itself full and fat. Then it loses its name.

The furthest thing from myth is description; I am ashamed of it for that very reason, I think.

You would like to pass freely and carelessly through the world, as though you never had any convictions. What do you care about being "in the right"? Do you want to live, or do you want to be "in the right"? You don't lack emotions, and you *hate* it when any kind of calculation is proven.

A person who escapes death because he has never heard a thing about it.

The disadvantage of religions: that they always speak of the same things. Perhaps this is one reason a lively mind like Stendhal's will hear nothing of religion.

A man who does not speak anymore, except for *statements that stay* with us.

A woman who knew all the great men and outlived them. One of them will not die. Her desperation.

Names—names in particular—need to be repeated. They are easily put into circulation, but they shouldn't stay in one place. One family, for example, can imperil a name. It can ingest the name completely, make so much use of it that for others it becomes empty and bloodless. A name within one family is shoved back and forth instead of rising up and taking flight. Among family members a name is never really let loose; it is burdened with habit as if with stones.

Religions that believe in their own *decline*. Fewer and fewer adherents belong, until there are just *four* left, as with the Jains.

His belief: that nothing is ever lost, particularly nothing that has taken place between people. The compulsion to rediscover everything that ever happened to a person, but always in relation to specific figures, never merely for itself, never outside the personal sphere. The changes in the places where events occurred turn into masks, and these masks are waiting to be seen through. We love these old places for their existence and hate them for their distortion.

Names, the most enigmatic of words. I have long been bothered by a sense, which has disturbed me more from year to year, that unraveling the enigma of the essence of names would provide the key to the process of history.

Just as the decoding of ancient scripts has brought vanished civilizations back to life, so too in the interpretation of names could be found the actual law of all that has been done by and to mankind.

Compared with this, the ominous depletion of numbers that started with Pythagoras would seem paltry and of limited import.

It is clear that all mythology depends on names. With myths, the name stays fresh. With religions, the name is depleted by its broad dispersion. The world religions account for the greatest possible depletion of names but are still bound up with them, even in their most diluted form. Mathematical thought, which has gradually led to human technological power, involves the abandonment of names; they are eliminated from the thought process, we think utterly without them.

Names, which intensify the strength of myth, now serve more the purpose of connecting.

Names as roots and names as vessels.

Names of low specific gravity: balloons, quickly lifting into the air. *Heavy* names that pull their bearers to the ground.

Name pairs, forming twinned masses.

The names of creatures are terribly important. The introduction of naming at the beginning of Genesis is one of the few clues to the nature of naming. The name of a person who died young, which he bore only a short time, is entirely different from an old person's name, long in use. Hungry names, sated names. The sudden fame surrounding hungry names. The fame of sated names in decline.

A man who is known by all but who knows no one. He never notices faces, voices, forms. When he has been loved by someone, he never knows who it was. He experiences the moment, but nothing remains of it. It seems to him that no one has a name or that everyone has the same name. People collect around him but run off him like water.

His pronouncements on this: "I don't notice differences. People are all the same. As for dogs—that's something else again."

He appears to be loveless but doesn't know hate either. He can have no grudges against anyone. He harms no one. This provokes many people to try to force their way into his memory.

Women's attempts to remind him of his relations with them. "I don't know," he always says, "it's certainly possible." You can take him anywhere—he doesn't care where he is. He is rented or robbed, used and abused. But in the long run no one can put up with his equanimity, and they always take him back to his home.

Because he is always saying, "It's all the same to me" or "Every man is the same," "Same" has become his name.

He is positively thriving, as though his lack of memory kept him young. Generations know him, talk about him, but he doesn't change; from father to son, from mother to daughter, it is always the same image of him that is handed down.

He is a tall, powerful man, his face set in a kind of permanent astonishment, never revealing any other expression. He approaches everyone quite openly, shying away from no one. He greets everyone with a trusting handshake. His trusting nature is like a child's, but in this archetype of a man it is irresistible.

While getting to know him, many mistrust him and try to uncover all sorts of dark secrets. But this always proves his innocence and eventually embarrasses even the most evil-minded doubter.

People like talking to him because he doesn't remember anything. He is the least dangerous of all father confessors. He has no possessions, but he has everything he needs. Everyone wants to be alone with him, and in this way he gets clothed and taken care of. He accumulates nothing: since he doesn't see anything as belonging to him, he gives it all away.

A woman's attempt to bind him to her through an

object of value. She brings him a beautiful gleaming ring, then she takes it away, bringing it back again every time she sees him. At last she thinks she can leave the ring with him. But on her next visit the ring has vanished. His household consists of the property of others. His benefactors are mindful of his minimal needs and keep things stored away for him.

Though he is often talked about, he never takes part in these discussions. To make him one's slave would be impossible since he obeys no one. At some point he must have learned speech; thus he cannot always have been without a memory. But since no one remembers this period, his background and his youth remain a mystery.

Animals approach him as if they were humans; it appears they get to know him.

Good people, always giving something away, until suddenly they bitterly regret it and hate everyone for it.

A voice that chirps, mercilessly.

The laugh of a pregnant woman: the child quickening within her.

It is a great pleasure to listen to people who have nothing to say. They ought to be what they are and not be judged for it; still less should one try to influence them. Keep your ears wide open and let it all flow in, in all its sense-lessness, disorder, and futility. You can make sense of it only later, in your own imagination.

He saw them as fishes swimming among one another, mouths of all sizes, totally at each other's mercy.

Elegant, well-curried words.

Torture: the hours lost listening to people who make the same confessions, year in and year out. A new person talking about himself for the first time always amazes us.

Brecht's preachiness as ersatz Bible proverbs: you need only to hold his sayings up against the power of the biblical ones he cites to see how dubious and poor his own are. Theater is not school, for it employs transformation as its most important method. Learning takes place only through the right kind of transformation—but this has not yet been found. Brecht objects to transformation because he knows and fears what it can do; thus his prohibition of it, his "alienation effect."

His life, in which nothing, absolutely nothing, happened. He embarked on no adventures, he was in no war. He was never in prison, he never killed anyone. He neither won nor lost a fortune. All he ever did was live in this century. But that alone was enough to give his life *dimension*, both of feeling and of thought.

The innocence of a person who has never murdered is precious. He will know till his last moment that he has killed no one. Let the murderers mock him! They will search heaven and hell in vain for those whom they killed. But they will never be granted the vengeance to which they would offer themselves up, and they will remain murderers for all eternity.

He laughs, out of forgetfulness.

Plato as the golden age of discourse. The conciseness of the Chinese.

She smiles at you, to laugh with the someone else.

His memory, like his heart, beating even in sleep.

A thought that swells with pride.

So it is not just the future that you want but a nobler future. Fine, why not? But what are you doing about it? Trying to smuggle your own words into it, to touch the future with your own self! What a ridiculous undertaking, what arrogance, what mindless, shameless, blind underestimation of the future!

He always sees the end in advance, so as not to begin anything.

I have never yet hated a man whom I did not feel sorry for later because the hate within me treated him so roughly.

He waits with bated breath for success, anywhere, under the earth, at the North Pole, on the moon.

Each individual perception is precious so long as it remains autonomous. But it dissolves into nothingness when absorbed into the gut of a system.

The couple's watches: never the same time.

Joubert has seriousness, grace, and depth. These three qualities share equally in his thinking, and thus he is closer to the ancients than any other aphorist. Of particular charm is his lack of weight. His melancholy does not burden his statements but rather seasons them with compassion and kindness. Even when attacked, he is not aggressive. His modesty does not allow for viciousness; his sense of the permanence of things keeps him from all that is petty. He breathes the spiritual as if it were air in motion. He senses thoughts and words as breath or as the ascent or descent of birds.

If we *really* knew what happens to our inmost thoughts, we would probably avoid ever having any.

All that blather about responsibility—and now, a few months later, you see what happens to your thoughts! But maybe the arrogance lies in your insistence on the form you have given to your ideas. But are they really *yours* then? Aren't you just one of many random transmitters? It is very hard not to take oneself seriously. Hard not to insist: I mean this and nothing else.

Don't tell me who you are. I want to worship you.

1961

❧ Your spirit has power only when it is given direction; left to its own devices, it would sing itself into despair.

How many people you have seen this week! The five historians from Berlin. The Italian actress from Australia. The young Jew from New York who worships Isaac Babel. The publisher with the most important voice in England. The mother of the deceased Otter woman. The secret hairdresser from the Abruzzi. Veza's weepy cavalier. The Chinese pianist and his fiancée, the daughter of the famous violinist. Kafka, who came from Frankfurt to ask for the hand of his cousin. It was a lot, it was too much, and yet you were nearly smothered by yourself alone.

Mercy is a flood that destroys him completely.

That which he could lose he casts far off from himself, to keep it in his possession.

To mangle a sentence into a landscape.

For months he didn't talk even to himself. Now words shoot out of him like knives.

We are hypocrites because we cannot forget the things we have acquired.

I would like once more to be as innocent as if I did not own a single book and hadn't written one yet.

Every forgotten idea crops up again on the other side of the world.

To have someone happy at home, so you can be happy elsewhere.

Sometimes things get so close that they ignite each other. This illumination, coming from closeness, is what we live for.

You have not even finally settled the few things you have thought about the last thirty years. Everything is all still there. The world is untouched; no one has figured it out. But there is enough within you now to create the world from yourself. You shrink from this because you still doubt your own breadth. "Is it even enough? Isn't it far too little?"

It is not important to tell oneself one is alone, when that's all it is. The pose of the solitary thinker makes his existence worthless. As for thinking something just because one is alone in thinking it, not to think it at all is better. One ought not to see oneself as here and the whole worthless world there. One may have to abstain from the world periodically, but this is happiness, not bitterness. Contempt for everyone one does not know, just because one does know some others, is an infallible sign of stupidity, and the worst of our human legacy.

Those things one tries to get to the bottom of disperse into nothingness. This is one danger. But they also become knottier. This is another danger: they become heavier, harder problems.

Learn to speak again at fifty-five, not a new language but speech itself. Discard all my prejudices, even if nothing else is left. Reread the great books whether I've actually read them before or not. Listen to people without lecturing them, especially those who have nothing to teach me. Stop validating fear as a means of fulfillment. Struggle against death without constantly pronouncing its name. In short, courage and justice.

Splendid to think that we are steeped in secrets. The nicest thing about learning is that it multiplies the secrets.

Whoever touches power will, unawares, be contaminated by it. He cannot forget it unless he can forget himself.

He cannot shut out loathsome praise; it crawls inside him and reaches his heart.

Uncanny how all the calculations agree, as though the universe arranged itself according to science.
   Subjection of the universe to the earth.

1962

His greatest satisfaction, which he constantly denies himself, is putting things in context.

He doesn't want to describe something, he wants to *be* that something. If he can't be it, he wants to sing its praises. If he can't praise it, then he wants to divine it.

Someone who always waits for the judgments of others. When suddenly they have none, he is subsumed by old opinions.

Indignation at being admired. That long, scornful nose of hers bounces men right off. She knows that she is beautiful only when she looks somber. The tragic aspect of her face would be likable without that weapon of a nose on it.

Even from their dearest beloved the dead vanish; in the end they even forget to call on them. It is better to live so intensely that no one can die.

I will never be convinced that there is a grandeur to kill-ing. I know what it feels like without myself having killed—it is worth less than a single breath of either the killed or the killer.

The hand that forms a single letter is mightier than the hand that kills; and the finger that has contributed to a death shall turn to dust before it has time to wither. As if it weren't enough that men die, without their abetting death!

There no man has ever seen another; even if he sees some-one daily, he does not recognize him. To recognize an-other person would be the most grievous insult. And this fiction is maintained in marriage. Thus, people do not have names; they feel freer without names. To be inde-pendent means to know no one. But since people can't entirely break the habit of memory, they conceal what they know, and it feels to them like guilt.

Both are following in his footsteps; soon enough they will be kicking each other.

He cursed his dream before all the leaves had fallen from it.

Perfection admits no one.

I was nothing but a will; now I am a sound.

The age of innocence has begun, when everything new quickly fades. The spirit is a ravenous beast no more; satiated with earlier prey, it now stays true to itself.

He has the consumptive illness called praise; he is already quite ravaged by it. Praise will gallop off with him to death.

Mosaic lyrics, made from hot pebbles.

The beautiful picture of Bettina, in which she appears as an old woman. Has she here become her beloved mother, who died in the camp? The picture was taken in the Lötschental by Bettina's husband, who last saw her mother in the camp and as her messenger came to Bettina and proposed. She became his wife and has been for fifteen years; now with the camera's help he has been able to transform Bettina into the likeness of her mother, whose final image he bore her in his gaze.

Wouldn't recurrence be even sadder than disappearance?

Every report of a planned, regular, recorded life fills you with guilt, and it seems to you as if you have wasted your whole life *staring at the clock.*

Happy when blowing into his Horn of Damnation, the Great Transformer.

Once he met a cleverer bird, capable, prudent, disciplined, and dreadfully practical. But, oh, how he prefers his own raven, foolish, obsessed, impulsive, and wonderfully boisterous!

You have to let words burst forth again—blind, evil, cruel, pitiless, and excessive—and not live in fear of every sentence coming into the hands of ten-year-old children. Responsibility is a sorry affair when it dogs your every step. Are you a king in Jukun or Ikara? You live in the jungle of *today's* people, all its people, and not in the well-mannered port of England.

He has spent so much time with extinct peoples that they know him on sight.

I no longer want anything *enough*. I want it a little, and hardly have I taken a step in its direction than I don't want it any more.

I am ashamed to seize an opportunity. That it is offered, that the opportunity exists, is nice—how can you then just grab it? If you're sure of it, you don't. Grab it, and you've lost it. But if you don't grab it, you may already have lost it—and that never occurs to me.

I am too old. I hate almost nothing. I have reached the stage where you like everything that's there. I am beginning to understand for the first time that there are philosophers who approve of everything in existence. To be sure, the disciples of death still fill me with revulsion. But I have not found an answer. I am faced with the same doubt I have always faced. I know that death is bad. I do not know what might replace it.

It is difficult to continue thinking about a book that now exists. So long as it was in manuscript, I could keep thinking about it. I was obligated by nothing. I had not, so to speak, signed off on anything. Now it is all in print: my ideas and yet not my ideas, something intermediate and embarrassing that somehow I will always have to admit to. I can only just connect with it, but I don't like connecting with myself—I only like to connect with things that are strange and new. So now I seem to myself like a hanged man dangling in the air, knowing and feeling that my own words are the noose.

Your original sin: you opened your mouth. As long as you listen, you are innocent.

His sentences rub against and so erase each other. This drives him to despair. So he makes of every sentence its own cage.

You must get back inside your head, into its storms, its northern lights, its conflagrations. Enough of this familiar veneer of civility, this incessant self-congratulation that you are alive. Are you, then? Are you learning? Doing anything? Getting bloody?

I am sick of longing for places I already have an image of. I am sick of being astonished by words because they are inscrutably splendid. I want to seek something that I, and only I, will find. I want to feel that nothing is certain until I have it. I can't bother with stones someone else has already piled up. Leave these games to the fair, who forget themselves in their self-assurance, to the dancers who only recognize themselves in front of mirrors, to the consumers, the travelers, the inheritors and celebrities.

Fear not your treasures turning to dust. They will decay only if you stand watch over them. Go ahead, quivering and uncertain. What you don't know will preserve what you do.

I went home and found a fez. Whose had it been? I put it on and went for a walk. Now everyone knew me. Soon I was a celebrity. The fez cast its crimson dignity about me. What was its purpose? There was general curiosity but never disrespect: all my pursuers kept their distance. I was disinclined to take off the fez; without it, everyone would have felt humiliated. I felt how I was exalting them all with my fez. If I had foreseen the fateful consequences, I would not have shown myself as much with it on.

The first several days I felt proud but calm. There was a certain positive tension, but it was containable. I did, though, note the anxious look an old woman gave me when her grandchild, an impressionable little girl, pointed her finger toward my fez and began to cry softly. I thought, she must *want* it, but I didn't dare kneel down for her to play with it. I bowed my head slightly, swaying the hat gently. At first the child was silent, then she burst into tears. Her sobs were heartbreaking, and I pulled away, embarrassed by the unseemly commotion she was making. I saw groups of people whispering on the other side of the square, but as I approached them they fell stonily silent. A dog put its tail between its legs and slunk away. A young woman fell to her knees in front of me and begged the fez for its blessing. How could I have withheld from her the very thing she so longed for? With a nod of my head I granted her wish; she clasped my knees and fell into a swoon. I was very moved, but got away somehow and left her lying there in bliss. How little, how little a human being needs. For him God can even take the form of a fez.

I so often agree with Tolstoy's way of thinking: how is it possible that his manner of expression disappoints and repels me? It irritates me that he forgoes *surprise*. For clarity and simplicity he states at the very outset how he will end things. The moral is there from the beginning; he never forgets it, nor does he change it. But he really ought to tell the story as if he had forgotten it and lost it; he should have forgotten it in the course of telling the story. Its sudden rediscovery would then be a revelation for the reader instead of being a storybook moral.

But one should not forget that he knew that most Russian people of his time were illiterate. So he may have viewed his task too broadly, deciding that he had to create books that would enable people to comprehend morality without outside help, each person for himself.

But he was also led astray by overplaying the significance of simple relationships. He liked to see people as *simple*, which they are not. Like all people, he was basically opposed to lies, to transformations. But this way of thinking ignores a major characteristic of humanity, and any further ideas that may be expressed are boring, as if meant for creatures who don't exist: the great advantage of the Greeks, whose learning starts with the *Odyssey*, a "lie" that here seems fortunate: namely, transformation.

Tolstoy cannot dictate laws to men since his whole critique of humanity is simply the residuum of his own past life, once rich and colorful. And it is just this, life's richness and color, that people will not be cheated of.

The day before yesterday, late: *Sonia*, a story reminiscent of Grimmelshausen. The father, a Hungarian landowner in Slovakia, the mother a Jew, three daughters (of whom I now know Enid and Sonia). The father always in his library. His talks with Sonia, the strongest daughter, during the second half of the war, his certainty of coming catastrophe. He sent two of his daughters to Budapest—Sonia studied agriculture at the university in Altenburg. Her last visit to the estate: she was never to return. Her parents' last postcard: "We are going to Komorn in a truck." A student who she knows is half-Jewish but who has false papers warns her she is in danger. Sonia demands to see her own papers and she gets them: her Jewish grandparents are there in bold underlining. The friendly student goes with her, first to Komorn, where she tries to get news of her parents. She learns that the only man who can tell her anything is the head of the local militia, a photographer. She tracks him down in his shop; he is in uniform. She asks about her father. "Baron Weiss? Sure, I remember him, he left four days ago." Not till much later does she learn what happened. The photographer was responsible for selection for transport. First the "intellectuals" were sorted out from the "manual laborers"; the latter were to be sent back home since there were no trains or trucks around. But first the Jews in the group were separated out; they would not be sent home. Her mother was with the Jews. Her father said, "Then I am going too." "By all means, if you like," said the photographer, and made note of Baron Weiss, the only non-Jew to go along of his own free will, so to speak. But then the women were separated from the men immediately. Her father ended up at Flossenburg, doing hard labor; he was killed there in December 1944. Her mother was sent to Ravensbrück; she was too weak to work. She died on January 12, 1945.

Sonia and the student left the photographer and started off for Budapest. In the next town there was a great hue and cry; she had strange premonitions and nearly fainted, without knowing why; then she heard that they were having a "Jew drive." She wanted to look among the people for her parents, but the student pulled her away: "Your parents have been gone four days." Sonia knew this, but the thought that she had somehow passed her parents by as they were being taken away never left her. The student accompanied her as far as Budapest and brought her to her sisters.

Later she heard about a position as chambermaid to the Archduchess Stephanie, the widow of Crown Prince Rudolf (she had married a Lonyai and now, age eighty, lived in the Orosvar Castle). "Her Royal Highness" wanted to emigrate to Switzerland and wanted a chambermaid who spoke languages to take along. Sonia made herself known to her, but the old lady didn't understand why she wanted the position. Sonia confided in her and found empathy: "She was not an anti-Semite." A week later Sonia started work; most of the castle was occupied by German soldiers, and she had to pass the sentry point. "That's sure no chambermaid." She pretended not to know German and got through. She was gradually trained in her duties by the archduchess, but already by the fifth day she had been entrusted with her mistress's wig; from then on she was indispensable. They were busy making preparations for the journey to Switzerland when the old lady had a stroke, and that was the end of travel plans. A German staff medical officer visited "Her Highness"; he went up to Sonia and declared, "You're no maid! Who are you? I want to help you!"

Sonia trusted him and told him her whole story. He told her that she was the subject of talk among the German soldiers in the castle, that they thought she was a Jew in hiding. He could help her only if he could say she was his lover. She agreed to this. He behaved honorably; in the course of the next week he confessed to her that he loved her. He was around fifty, married, he had children but his wife did not understand him. When the Russians came, the Germans vacated the castle; he wanted to stay for her sake, if she would agree to marry him later. They discussed the idea at length and came to the decision that he could not stay. He left, and she stayed behind, in great consternation.

As the Russians approached, a priest (a Benedictine who happened to be at the castle) gathered all the women and girls, to wall them in (and thus protect them from the Russian soldiers). But Sonia had to stay with the archduchess. The Russians arrived, and on hearing that an old princess was living in the castle, they wanted to have a look at her. They were expected any minute in the old lady's sickroom, and to save Sonia the priest hit upon the idea of having her hide in the old lady's bed. Still clothed she crawled under the covers and squeezed up against the wall. Now came the parade of Russians; one after the other they filed politely by the bed of the "princess" and looked at her curiously. While they were plundering all over the castle, here in the room of the "princess" they touched nothing. The priest received them all and did the honors, so to speak. They did not touch him; it was simply not true that the Russians were after aristocrats, priests, or other Hungarians. They were looking only for German soldiers and, when they were drunk, for women.

After they had left the sickroom, she thought she was saved. But when night came, she heard a drunken Russian in the courtyard below. He was yelling that he knew the chambermaid was there, hiding in the bed of the "princess." He came upstairs, she squeezed more tightly against the wall, she heard his steps approaching, all at once he pulled the covers from off the archduchess, and she saw a machine gun pointed at her. In her shock she forgot everything that had gone before, even the name of the German staff doctor, and in the seventeen years since, she has wracked her brain for his name, unable to remember it again. She got up from the bed and followed the Russian, the whole time under threat of the machine gun. Now I have only two choices, she thought to herself, to die or to give in. Suddenly in the long corridor the roll call started. Fighting was still going on: the Russian left her standing there and ran to his unit. Russians could plunder and take women, but when the roll call was read, they had to obey instantly or be shot. So she was saved; a miracle, said the priest, a true miracle.

She stayed a while longer at the castle; Archduchess Stephanie's condition went rapidly downhill. The priest bought a horse for Sonia, and she rode for four days to Budapest. During those four days the value of the horse increased tenfold. She sold it immediately on arriving, and here she was lucky, for two hours later she would not have been able to sell it. From this windfall her two sisters lived for six months. That was what I heard of her story. Much more would have followed, but it had gotten so late I had to stop, and she had to go to bed. I have told only the most important parts, and in abbreviated form, and the story has lost all its color. When I visit her in Paris, I hope to hear more.

Interpreting a statement's meaning—all that remains of the tradition of consulting oracles. But since this takes place outside the scope of fear, not even that is left.

The true stories that we tell are false; with false stories at least there is the chance that they might come true.

All our lives we circle around the same ideas, as if they were so many suns. So why should we not at least hope for comets?

The progress of friends who include us in their progress: nothing makes us feel lonelier and more alien.

How much it bothers him when he recalls something, but with the wrong people. It makes even the realest memories false, and they cry out like stuck pigs.

One book! Three-fourths of your life is there—your hope, your pleasure, your melancholy, your sorrow, and your doubt. All of that you have now lost. Where are you? What is left of you? The crater your book left.

A man who delights in touching every woman because she will never be his.

The French: they sit down for dinner as if for life everlasting.

Since visiting Greece, I read the Greeks differently: more haltingly, as if going from name to name; more easily, as if my visit were still to come.

Never to see again the highest beauty.

After Paris: to find my way back to the Chinese, my greatest joy. And if it takes me the whole winter, I want to be with the Chinese and stay there. With them, all the forms of my own thinking are more clearly outlined. I feel myself unfolding, opening up around them. Nature and custom have their full meaning. The spirit has not sucked life dry. Life is everything; it is ready and waiting for every transformation. Not even Buddhism has smothered China in spirituality. Nor will the narrow modernists be able to. And I know I need China more than I need my bread.

The brevity of Chinese books: I'd like to be, and stay, that brief.

The parallel reader. He has ten books open at once and reads *one* sentence in each, then the next sentence in the book beside it. What a scholar!

Have you listened to all this music only to succumb to the voices of those entirely unknown to you?

You are a simple man, you put your trust in few ideas, but in those completely.

A beast that has lived since the beginning of creation.

"Quel dérèglement de jugement, par lequel il n'y a personne qui ne se mette au-dessus de tout le reste du monde, et qui n'aime mieux son propre bien, et la durée de son bonheur, *et de sa vie*, que celle de tout le reste du monde!"
(The survivor)

Pascal

If prayers were to be answered, they could not be retracted: a highly alarming state of affairs.

"The human race uses thought only as an evasive tactic."
from Conversations with Goethe

1964

A man's wife dies. Now he has no one. He knows a young woman who lives far from him, half a continent away. He calls her every night. She speaks with him, they have long talks together. He no longer wants to talk to anyone living closer. Being in communication with her night after night from this distance makes him feel hopeful about his dead wife. Now he does nothing during the day, he just waits for the night. When he can't get through or she isn't home yet in the evening, a fearful desperation comes over him. She alone can calm him, but only at this remove. When she is closer to him he does not know who she is. He tells her everything, every night, and talks with her for hours and hours. He has his wife's ashes, letters, and pictures in his home, and he knows very well that it is not she with whom he converses. The speaker is far younger, her voice is different, she comes from a totally different country. He never confuses her with someone else, he knows her as well as he does himself, and her moods are as familiar to him as his own. He listens to her, responds, listens more, sometimes gets impatient with her when she has nothing to say or takes too long to say it, and makes threats. It is not easy to say what he threatens her with. For even when he says he won't call her for a few days, they both know better.

To make a secret of waiting so no one in the world knows about it except the person expected and the person waiting—an emotion exceeding all others in intensity. And when love is involved, especially love at great distances, say requiring a plane trip from one continent to another, then the final arrival is the greatest happiness human beings can experience, for that other joy, which would be even greater, the return of the dead, is denied them.

The question of belief, which has always occupied me, which I have wanted to resolve, and whose center I am now plunged into. Things are such that my life depends on my belief in a certain person. But nothing is as difficult for this particular person, who is by nature a poet, as "truth." I am confronted, so to speak, with the self that I once was; and from this person, who is a kind of deputy of myself, I must force the absolute truth. But he is totally incapable of it. I need belief where I know I cannot find it, and the old obsession that has plagued me for decades is replaced by a new one, no less hopeless: belief. But this way I can still get closer to the nature of belief: by observing and noting every phase of this struggle for it. For my insight into its hopelessness takes nothing away from its seriousness.

The young yield to every impression in order not to be obsessed by anything. Are they right? Is this kind of person more natural? Are they the forerunners of future generations without beliefs? Are they the only ones to have gotten rid of the biblical God? We might think so if we didn't know that they, too, can become a crowd, just as irretrievably as we, as irretrievably as everyone before us.

To say the most horrible thing such that it is no longer horrible; it gives one hope because it was said out loud.

But there are days too much enriched at the expense of other days, days filled retroactively with the years that came after, to the point that less is left of these years than of those days. We should eradicate these forged days.

"History" is made of these forged days.

Diaries which are too accurate are the end of freedom. Thus we should keep them only intermittently, so that the "empty" intervals become the fullest entries.

The sufferer whom people admire because he never forgets himself.

Why? he says to himself, why do I walk this road when there are a hundred thousand others? Are they all really so similar that it doesn't matter? Or is this road so special that I would go wrong on all the others? He will never know; but for fifty years he will continue on this road, sure and certain of his goal, one man, one pace.

A man whom all abandon so he can learn to be silent.

Yesterday this story of a young German woman's search for her father's remains. Her mother, brother, boyfriend, and she drive from northern Germany to Collioure in Roussillon, on the Spanish border, where her father, who had been called up toward the end of the war into the field corps, was captured and died. He was taken to a prison camp in February 1945 and died at the end of the year. He did not know what had happened to his family, and vice versa. Late in 1946 they received a card saying "Décédé." Four years later, from Paris, someone sent them his briefcase with scraps of paper on which he had occasionally written notes. On his daughter's birthday he had embossed her name on a piece of metal; she was nine then. The four traveled to Collioure in 1957 and looked up one of his prison guards. North of Perpignan they also found the cemetery where more than five hundred German prisoners of war were buried. There was his grave and his name. He had never previously traveled farther than Bavaria, where he had hiked on the Zugspitze with his wife. His imprisonment was his only foreign southern vacation.

The young woman now has an eleven-month-old child, and she keeps the scrap of metal that her father embossed with her name hidden in her home. She hardly dares to look at it and has hidden it so well that all of a sudden she will forget where she put it and will live in mortal fear that it is lost. At which point she conducts a complete search of her entire, very large apartment; on finding it, she immediately hides it again.

He positively hisses with kindness. To what avail? Nobody believes such grimacing.

Praise of one's rival as self-praise: Stravinsky on Schoenberg.

Don't seek the silent syllables within yourself; you will find them only in the babbling of others.

Self-satisfied: a self worn out.

Orestes: Euripides

Read Euripides' *Orestes* today. Reaffirms for me that in every way Greek tragedy deals with death. The variations are countless, from murder to death to lament. The originality, the invention of the dramas, depends on where they begin. In this case, Orestes and Electra are just about to be stoned to death, the people of Argos will judge them, and they await the verdict without much hope. Later Pylades joins them, wanting to die along with them. Remarkable, the last-minute plot to murder Helen: the idea of taking vengeance on her, for whom so many Greeks have fallen.

On first reading, her removal by the god Apollo, at the point of greatest danger, appalls me. (She is transported to the realm of the gods, there to live in eternal bliss.) The justification he gives for this: she was just the instrument of the gods, who used her to set the Greeks and the Trojans on one another. Humans were too wicked and there were too many of them, so what Helen brought about was also in line with the gods' intentions. It ends up in a ghastly happy ending. Orestes marries the daughter of the very Helen whom he had just threatened to murder.

If these scenes are not the scorn of a god hater, then they make no sense. No diatribe against the gods could be more affecting. Granted that at the last moment Apollo saves Orestes, whom he had incited to matricide. In the logic of the play, Apollo brings on a kind of apotheosis at the end. But with the end of Helen, with the end of the Trojan War, in the house of the murdered Agamemnon the full measure of the gods' wickedness is taken, and fairest Helen is now one of them.

Helen: Euripides

The action takes place at the grave of Proteus. At Hera's behest, the real Helen has been abducted to Egypt and has been living there for seventeen years. Everything that has occurred meanwhile at Troy actually involved an apparition of Helen, her double, with whom Menelaus has now begun the journey home. A shipwreck lands him on the coast of Egypt, and he encounters the true Helen dressed in rags. She is being wooed by the king of the country, Proteus's son, but she resists him; for this reason he threatens death to any Greek who lands. When Helen and Menelaus recognize each other, there is only one way for them to escape: they say that Menelaus is dead. Menelaus, himself in rags, plays the messenger of his own death, and Helen convinces the enemy king that she can become his wife under one condition, that a shipboard funeral for Menelaus be held on the open sea. Then she will be free to become the barbarians' queen. For the funeral sacrificial offerings, she and the false messenger (in fact, Menelaus) are granted a ship with oarsmen. They both board the ship, along with the shipwrecked Greeks, who have been hiding on the coast. Once on the high seas the crew is overpowered and the couple escape.

The crux of the drama is a living person who is pronounced dead and plays the part of another against his enemy, a new variation on the central theme of Greek tragedy. Since the hero is really alive and the reports of his death are feigned, the outcome is positive.

This "appearance" of the dead Menelaus is a curious extension and reversal of the apparition of the false Helen, who has hardly left the scene when it is decided that Menelaus is no longer alive. Only thus can he win back the real Helen and return home with her.

The Trojan War and all that came after it was no more than a continuation of the intrigue between Hera and Aphrodite. The actions of the gods are emotionally less offensive to us when we see the gods simply as the true powers that still hold sway over our earthly rulers. They are no different from them; they have the same characteristics and treat kings just as kings treat their own subjects and slaves. But they have also decided on war, because there are too *many* mortals.

For J.-M., every woman is more than any man, even the lowest, most hard-bitten outcast of a woman, and without hesitating he would throw a genius to a whore to devour and still fear he had wronged *her*. His Christianity, his humility, his feeling of being a sinner make him put all women in the right, because he is a man.

If you were a hundred years old, you would be so well understood that everything would be wrong again.

I know nothing, and I know least of all what I have found out myself.

What does this mean? That I must find it out again? Or that it only has meaning when *others* rediscover it?

1965

To find your spiritual unity again, to *know* what you are thinking about, to pry figures from the dreams of decades, consort with them, entrust your life to them, lose your fear of them.

I have read my old sentences again; they are no longer mine. Since they were printed a piece of my life has fallen away from me.

The public sucks the blood from a man's soul, and what is left is just a shadow, which bows down to them.

False acquaintances and expectations still surround him like a wall of vileness. Until it collapses not a single truth will be granted him.

To bring past years to present moments.

The young person, delighted by the countless idiotic remarks he is allowed to make—suddenly he sees his great future before him.

(83)

Loneliness, the sword we draw against those who love us. The cruelty that horrified me in Picasso was my own; still, he was able to protect her from himself with his enormous activity. But I? With what?

Behind every woman he likes talking to he sees a literary figure. He surrounds himself with the elect society of such people. It is obvious he hasn't a clue about real people. His life is led exclusively in the conceptual realm, and his only passion is getting ahead. A thinker who can't start from the concrete is no thinker for me, and a single fragment, a single phrase of a Greek philosopher of whom nothing else survives is more to me than all the works of the living A.

A thinker must forget that he is clever, else no matter what the field he will think only about his own cleverness.

What happens to names in all their relations? The sole accomplishment of certain minds is pulling together all sorts of names. While this might come naturally and gradually to most people, these types do it with force. It cannot be denied that in this way things sometimes come about that might not have otherwise.

For names are spiteful and greedy and cannot leave each other alone for a moment. They bite off whole chunks of each other like the most predatory fish. They sense, more than see, each other's presence. It is unthinkable that they could quietly look at one another. They are potentates, pretentious and irreplaceable, and their pervasiveness makes them more dangerous.

An insecure name is not a name, or it is felt to be a freak by the others. When exposed, some names get frightened and try to hide. If they can, they gather strength in darkness and become invincible. Other names, swallowed whole by bigger ones, prove indigestible. The time can come when they are all that remains of their predator, for, like a dangerous parasite, they have destroyed him from within.

One might ask what makes man so addicted to names, why he becomes a slave to them, inside and out.

A conversation about a name we know absolutely nothing about. The way it comes up in the conversation (which we overhear), how often and when it is mentioned again, after having been just "he" for a while.

We write because we cannot speak out loud to ourselves. Speaking to others leads to the most unpredictable estrangements. They gradually lose their own separate existence because of all the countless words with which we attack and overpower them. A kind of slow murder, it is among the most terrible things in human life. It is like someone's pressing down to close off our air passages but taking years until we stop breathing entirely. We stay more innocent when we write.

"I know what you mean." A catchphrase of this psychologizing time, really signifying that we have given up trying to understand the other person before we have even heard him. For we have understood everyone before they have even said a thing.

It is necessary that we leave our learning alone from time to time, that we put it away, not use it, almost forget it. It is precisely this compulsive quality of much learning that makes it necessary to let air into it, loosen it, fill it with the breath of years. It can be part of our nature only when it has given up its compulsiveness.

Most people say "God" to hide from themselves.

Love: a snake with two heads that unceasingly keep watch on each other.

A person is good even when all praise him for being so.

A country where everyone walks backward, to keep an eye on themselves. A country where all turn their backs on one another: fear of eyes.

First, only misunderstandings are left. These will die away; then the work will remain.

A labyrinth made of all the paths one has taken.

She can forget the same thing a hundred times: how he envies her that!

A man who on his own must make up for all the wars he once evaded.

His timidity about bringing any more hopelessness into the world, even by the most honest work, has grown insuperable. How does he differ from Gogol, with his flaming fears?

You have described so many things that move you. Have you left out the most important?

That raving maniac in Munich, placing the hope of the world on Alexander and the *diadoches* (relief troops), on Augustus.

In Nestroy, you think, you have all Austria. You are deceived; in him you have the delight one finds in malice.

The special interconnection of the social classes in Nestroy, more clearly outlined than anywhere else. Flattery and guile, the *forms* flattery takes, and the schemes of double-crossers.

Words in Nestroy that I never even knew were Austrian, many of my naive and natural words—I read in the notes with astonishment what they mean.

In the sixth book of the life of Apollonius of Tyana the discussion of the animal gods of Egypt. Apollonius attacks the naked Ethiopians' ways and derides their animal gods. This angers them, and in response they argue that the customs of the Greeks (the scourging of young men in Sparta) seem to them absurd and undignified. They cannot decide on this point and no one's mind is changed.

What I like in the account of Apollonius's life is the unbroken variety of gods, despite many echoes of Christianity (contempt for money, violence, and sex).

What I don't like are all the stories of his second sight. This was probably crucial to the godlike qualities ascribed to him. There are intellectual miracles of a different sort from Christ's, showing off his philosophic superiority: Apollonius always knows best.

In this role he meets secular rulers on an equal level, even Romans like Vespasian, Titus, and Domitian. Far from despising power, he wants to influence it for good.

His falling out with Euphrates, one of his closest and most important pupils, is traced to Euphrates' love of money. This quarrel has disturbing aspects, and though Euphrates' villainy is held accountable as far as the argument is concerned, we are never quite convinced of Apollonius's greater virtue.

A drama that overplays the differences in size among people. People are as different from one another as if they were dogs.

The avaricious, who conceal themselves so well that eventually they disappear.

How much we can ask of *one* person simply because we despise the others.

A.'s art: to say as much as possible as cleverly as possible for as long as possible, without ever saying one word that really strikes the spirit. So I loathe him even more than if he had nothing to say at all.

The infusion of Platonism in Cervantes is interesting only in the places where it becomes negative. When ideas are delusion, they lose the hollow, worn-out falseness they have accreted in the course of an overlong literary tradition. Of course, this is the great thing about Don Quixote: the idea and the ideal as madness, in all its consequences, uncovered and skewered. Whether this is ridiculous or not is not the issue: to me it seems terribly serious.

The moral quality of Cervantes is his desperate attempt to cope with the wretched circumstances of his daily life, his conforming to the official conventions of the powers of his time. This is why he is careful that virtue wins out and why he behaves like a Christian. Fortunately his substance, the misery of his real life, is so immeasurably great that conformism could never quite smother it.

Tremendous affection for Cervantes because he knew better than the conventional wisdom of his age and because his hypocrisy, which perhaps he himself didn't see through, is nonetheless transparent. I admire his *spatial* breadth; his fate, which so drove him hither and yon, gave him breadth instead of lessening him. Also I love the fact that he became known so late and that despite, or even because of, this he never gave up hope. Despite the many falsifications of life that he allowed into his "ideal" tales, he loved life as it is.

For me, this is the sole criterion of the epic talent: a knowledge of life even at its most horrific, a passionate love for it nonetheless, a love that never despairs, for it is inviolable even in its desperation. Nor is it really tied to a belief, for it originates in the variety of life, its unknown, astonishing, wondrous variety, its unpredictable twists and turns. For those who cannot stop pursuing life, it changes in the pursuit into a hundred new, overwhelmingly remarkable creatures; and for those who just as tirelessly chase after all hundred of them, they will change into a thousand others, all just as new.

The superior "higher" people in Cervantes' novellas are no less "high" than in Shakespeare. But it is welcome when, in Cervantes, the children of these higher characters run off for at least a few years of "low" living. The young nobleman who for love becomes a gypsy (though his lover turns out not to be a gypsy after all) or the young man in "The Highborn Barn Maid" who bolts for freedom, returning three years later without his upper-class parents' suspecting where he really was. If we could only know what lies he tells them before running off again! With Cervantes, love is really a "lowlife" concern, but to become famous for knowing it so well, he sets the "high" impossibly high, to flatter those who could be his patrons. But there is more here than mere flattery: he would rather *be* in their shoes. Should we think it lucky that his wretched lot never did improve?

We really cannot say. The effect of privation on invention is different with everyone, and without knowing the person at hand well, we will never know whether there was too much or too little of it, whether it helped or hindered the power of invention.

A person escapes fame by changing names but gets more famous with every one.

As long as I am writing I feel safe. Perhaps I write for just that reason. But it doesn't matter what I write. It's important only that I not stop. It can be anything as long as it is for me, not a letter or something imposed or required from outside. But if I have not written for a few days I become confused, desperate, down, vulnerable, mistrustful, threatened by a hundred perils.

I know that everything is *changing*, and because I feel the ineluctable coming of the new, I turn to the old wherever I can find it. It might be that I just want to save and preserve it because I can't bear the passing of anything. But it could also be that I am testing it, to use against death, still unbeaten.

Other writers have written memoirs. Memoirs attract me too. I just find it hard to take them seriously enough, given the omnipresence of death.

Perhaps, too, I fear diluting the seriousness and sincerity of my thinking by revealing its sources in my life. It is unimportant how I have arrived at something that concerns everyone as well as myself. So I would need to write memoirs in a way that would reinforce my convictions in the eyes of others. I still mistrust the selective cleverness of any new insight. Thus, I don't pay enough attention to formal speculations on the renewal of an art form that once was my own. They seem like game playing. I like games well enough but I don't want to forfeit any of my real goals to them. I could try saying: Forget death for a year and use this year for everything you have neglected on account of it. But can I? Can I really?

The figure of a lover who suddenly is struck with the horrible realization that others are lovers too. The minute he can no longer deny the truth of this, as soon as he *sees* it, his own emotion dissolves.

The variety of Stendhal's travel books. His apodictic pronouncements and judgments. His passion for fictional national characteristics and for famous people. His even greater passion for victims and women. His naiveté: not one of his emotions embarrasses him. His love of disguises, at least in names. We like him because he *says* it all. He doesn't try to make every little thing conform to his own vanity. Though full of reminiscences, Stendahl doesn't get bogged down in them. His reminiscing has that rarest quality, open-endedness. He is always finding something new because he loves all kinds of things. He is often delighted. No matter what his good fortune, he never feels guilty. He doesn't tire us with long discussions, because he hates the theoretical. His thinking is lively, but he sticks to that which he himself has felt. He does not live without gods, but they come from all kinds of spheres, and it never occurs to him to relate them by family or marriage. He sees cities only if he finds people in them. He doesn't let a good story go untold. He writes a great deal, but is never pompous. The absence of religion keeps things light.

Stendhal was not my bible, but among writers he was my savior. I have certainly not read all of him, let alone more than once. But I have never opened anything by him without feeling light and bright. He was not my law. But he was my freedom, and whenever I felt smothered I found it in him. I owe him far more than I owe those who influenced me. Without Cervantes, without Gogol, Dostoyevsky, Büchner, I would be nothing, spirit without fire or contour. But I could live only because there is Stendhal. He is my justification and my love of life.

I will never succumb to adjectives, especially in threes. They are Proust's Orientalism, his love of jewels. These say nothing to me, for I love all stones. The "precious" stones for Proust are the aristocrats among his characters. My "aristocrats" are those unknown people of "the beginning": bushmen, Aranda, Tierra del Fuegans, the Ainu. My "aristocrats" are all those who still live by myths, who would be lost without them. (And now they are, mostly.) The society in which Proust made his way, his snobbishness, was his way of experiencing the world. That world leaves me cold. I am only interested in it when I read him or Saint-Simon.

All the people we have known return under new names, in unexpected circumstances. We look at them questioningly, hopefully: don't they recognize us, since we recognize them?

Perhaps people are able to distinguish only among a discrete number of faces, and when that number is exceeded, perhaps after a certain age they are receptive only to the old faces they already know, and in the new see only those.

Every sharp mind soon oppresses us, makes us ashamed, as if we had broken a promise. But regardless, every mind properly exists for itself, even an "inferior" one that hasn't quite reached such refinement.

She said that even the English can show grief about death and gave me many examples of mourning for dogs.

Since he went into mourning he no longer knows who his friends are.

This aversion to modern literature that you don't like to admit—an aversion to modern man.

Memoirs of the Florentine world traveler Carletti. He started at age eighteen as a slave trader with his business-man father in the Cape Verde Islands, sailed with his first cargo to Cartagena and then to Panama, Lima, Mexico, Manila, Japan, and Macao, where his father died. He met another Florentine there, in whose company he spent more than a year. Then he journeyed back via Ceylon and India, and near Saint Helena his ship was captured by

Dutch pirates and taken to Zeeland. There he fought in court for years to reclaim his stolen possessions but met with little success, and finally, fifteen years after he left, he returned to Florence, where he told the grand duke about his journey. He saw much that was interesting, but his narration seems somehow pale, warmed-over: the thing that interested him the most was prices. A true merchant, and the forerunner of today's tourists, who mainly record and convert the prices in foreign countries. Having lost all his journals, he reports everything from memory: he still has all the prices in his head, citing them everywhere, and it is quite possible that they were the chief point of interest for his grand duke as well.

All that's left of him are bones—but the noise they make! The bustle, the bother, the disturbance! With them alone he wants to accomplish what his flesh never could: his bones should grow rich and famous.

The oracle: he loves his own confusing inconsistency. He has succeeded in making an art of it. He fears nothing so much as losing it. He is his own cog in the wheel of time, and puts all his hopes in his inconsistency. Eventually, maybe, half sentences will have some kind of meaning.

He keeps people in subjugation, the better to despise them. These fools, who still believe or are bound to some belief, give him the strength to keep up the ragged show of confusion. For each one of them he has a word prepared, one that doesn't fit with any other. He maintains that no man has ever understood what another has said; if men only understood this, they would be better off.

But as it is, they hang on every strange word and poison their lives with whatever they suppose it means. He likes to listen when others miscommunicate. It delights him to recreate their helplessness. They suspect that he might hear confession, but he won't hear anyone alone. If two people come and confess to each other simultaneously, however, he is all ears. His patience is infinite when they reveal to him their confusion. Then he smiles, friendly and cheering, saying over and over, "And then? And then?" Nothing bores him, nothing seems too long, so long as what he hears satisfies his passion to know.

It has happened that four or even eight people have appeared before him at once. He doesn't refuse them; he is particularly attracted by the fact that they think they know one another and come as a group. He notes very quickly where their lines of division run and discreetly sets himself up as the ringmaster of their disunity. Some, who expect the opposite of him, are against him: these he quickly silences. It is so easy to expose their abysmal absurdity, and in one another's presence they are even more easily shamed. He records his triumphs in short, nasty phrases.

What do the clever know of how much effort and cunning it takes not to succumb to the paranoia that is his natural tendency. How stubbornly he must struggle against his *integrity*, as others do against disintegration; how tireless and artful he has to be in distracting his mind so that it doesn't focus on madness and evil; how he must divide himself up a thousand times to have enough breath to take in the world; how he tortures those he loves, because he loves them more intensely; how careful he must be not to see through things, because this destroys them for him; how he must keep on fighting death, the enemy, for only it has the universality to contain everything he hates.

F. sees reason in everything that is. Every institution makes sense; deftly his thought will find and administer its justness. He is peaceable and gentle; he doesn't like fighting. Instead of weapons he relies on institutions. He compares but never attacks—there are so many sides to every issue that there is nothing left to attack. Tolerance keeps him away from religion: priests are as repugnant to him as soldiers. And he will say so of the former, but on the latter he is silent. He is ashamed of his cowardice but rather proud of his tolerance.

At home he is the opposite of a father. Certainly he loves his children, but he despises the authority every father has and he is reluctant to make use of it.

Books are his great passion: their appearance, their publication dates, prices, authors, reviews, and contents. Somehow he knows them, even if he can't read them, since his profession doesn't leave him much time for reading.

He really knows pictures and loves many of them with an awkward tenderness.

He is so loyal to the dead that they can never really disappear. He moves back toward them; they light up within him like pictures. In his eyes there is a grief that he will never give words to. But it was always there, even before their deaths, as if he had always known.

He is reserved, but he needs others who are not. In his youth, he was ill-used by moralistic pronouncements. So, while he hates intolerance, he has the acutest moral reactions to people.

He is tall and very thin; his limbs move about like snakes and drape themselves around chairs and other furniture. They are never still, constantly arranging themselves in new patterns.

Old friends are exciting, for we can know an infinite amount about them and see it all right there at once, and it seems to be more than could ever fit into one person.

Disturbing, this overflow in people we know for a long time—we could drown in it.

But we seldom think of all we know about people. We have forgotten most of it, and what remains is false, so we are as fresh for them as on the first day.

Memorial days: where misunderstandings intersect.

I am sick of these conversations with myself. I want to direct the conversations of others.

The "Notes" make most suspect the notion that everyone chooses something completely different for himself and then copies what someone else chose.

It's against his nature to be a critic—he is too grateful.

Astounding, when things we recited to ourselves so often suddenly turn out to be true.

Hatred of destruction of any kind becomes dangerous itself: as reverence for *everything* that exists, the best as well as the worst.

You have to attack yourself so devastatingly that it's really not fun. Without serious injuries that leave scars, you shouldn't be allowed to get up again.

The animals he uses to ornament his thoughts curse him in silence.

Probably all satirists are one and the same person.

The evil eye I had no longer interests me. But I am enchanted when I read others who have it.

1966

❧ Someone who can say nothing out loud without its coming true.

Contempt for one's fellows must be balanced with self-contempt. If the latter prevails, then the writer is lost: he will destroy himself like Gogol. If the former prevails, the result is a prophet: arrogantly certain in his belief, he is a threat to the world, and thus ecstatically he helps bring about its destruction.

Finding the right balance.

Through the novels I finally allow myself to read, I animate the thousand figures and situations slumbering uneasily within me. Every book worth reading touches on a different part of life. I must do *this*, I tell myself today; I must write about *that*, I say tomorrow. Where should I begin, with so much waking at once? But still, if more quietly, I feel the suspicion that it is not right to work on something that was just my life. Isn't it really unimportant *who* is recalling? And are sheer memories worth preserving, as if they could stand for the memories of others? And so one longs for the time when nothing was experience as yet, when everything was intuition. Only the poets who died young—Büchner, Trakl—maintained the purity of their expectations. For all the others, expectations were gradually transformed into experience. In this one respect it can be said that Kafka always stayed the same; from the beginning he had the integrity and wholeness of his old age, and he was spared the fate of getting young later on.

But that is exactly what has happened to me. I had the wisdom of old age in the intuitions of my youth. Now, at sixty, I am catching up with the foolishness of youth.

Perhaps this is the odd excitement I should be writing about, but it feels uncanny to me and I don't trust it. And I haven't yet found the formal medium that would serve as a legitimate structure for it.

Perhaps I am striving too much for a lost unity; perhaps—even in my work—I should let my self disintegrate into its component parts.

As soon as I concern myself with one of these parts, I have hardly begun when the others quickly announce themselves: "We are here too. Remember, you are writing a forgery if you leave us out." And so I am scared off and keep waiting for a way to open up so as to handle them all at once.

Good old would-be father of the race! Wanted to have five hundred sons and got only one, himself . . .

He reveals himself as a member of all existing parties, collecting them, always finding new ones.

"Folklore" sounds like a parrot that belongs to everyone at once, to all the "folk."

More talkative in solitude.

To see how writers are derived from specific painters, a new branch of literary criticism.

Thus we see that every name has the potential to become famous, as long as it doesn't exceed a certain number of syllables.

Dante's project appears to me to be ever more monstrous. Who could emulate him and call together the names of *our* time before such a bar of justice as his poem is? Today the hardest thing to manage is merely to judge *oneself*, and how proud one is just to succeed honestly in that!

No one has the integrity and trustworthiness of a judge anymore.

The judge is suspect even to himself. We don't believe that he is a judge; we don't believe he isn't ashamed of it. This shame is the creation of Kafka.

If it really matters to you, get mad when you say it, or say nothing. Take off your gloves, and don't come on too softly: it should wake you up, after all.

I so long to get free of the things that have stamped me and all the thinkers of our time and to ponder death as "impartially" as if I were a man of the previous century.

With friends we should keep an old-fashioned kind of distance, as if the telephone did not exist.

The people we don't miss we have seen too much of; there's nothing more to be done about it.

She speaks from the navel.

What if it were all just an overture and no one knew to what?

He sank three times, but to no avail—no one saw him. The fourth time he stayed up and no one saw him then either.

He wrote down everything God reported to him, hot off the press.

What a poet doesn't see never happened.

A stranger: when he opened his mouth wide to yawn, I recognized him.

You are distinguished by an almost mythic pedantry; you need your monstrous exaggerations to be true.

He was a mountain and erupted. He was a tree and toppled. He was a lion and lost heart.

How much we think and will never comprehend!

Word associations: only interesting if you leave out five of six connecting links.

She laughs as if some one were tickling her, not in the right places but just slightly off.

The kindly schoolmaster who steals from his students but always just from the best.

The wiseguy from New York. He can't speak a word of English.

Literature of leaps and literature of steps.

Wales. I've been in strange and beautiful places the last five days, being shown much and seeing a good deal more. The ancient language, which I did not understand but heard everywhere, has a stubbornness and strength. But in order to save it—it is waging a desperate fight for survival—the people who speak it are constantly aware of it. They point with pride to every famous man who came from their midst, saying, "He was one of us," and perhaps it does not really matter what he was famous for. Words mean everything to them—more than a sacred scripture, they have a sacred tongue. They cling to every scrap of land that is still theirs, they cling to their dead.

I didn't hear any *preaching* in this language. Occasionally, when in longer conversations I would get excited, I felt the heightened attention of others, as if they sensed some link in me to their preachers.

The most wonderful things were the call of the curlews and the huge trees in the garden.

The humility of trees: that we can *plant* them, that they grow at our behest, where we want them to be.

My friends showed me everything, their entire history, from the cloister at the university in Bangor, where they met, to the little registry office in Bala, where they got married, to the village houses where Eirwen lived during the war, waiting for her husband's leave, to the country road where late one night, extremely pregnant, she got caught in a thunderstorm.

The ancient farm of their friends who spoke English only with effort. The clock inside always an hour ahead. The eighty-year-old farmer, hands spotted with paint, coming home after nine from a sheepshearing at a neighboring farm. He had worked all day; they had shorn a thousand sheep.

Earlier, at supper, his son-in-law tells stories, with the emphasis of a Japanese actor; he has a face like a fox, but his eyes are piercing and kindly like those of a saint.

His exceedingly fat wife runs out of the kitchen, in rapid succession tosses various dishes onto the table, and before the guest has quite finished what was on his plate, hops up, insisting clumsily in her high-pitched voice that he help himself right away, eat, eat.

Afterwards she hauls out of the top drawer photographs that show the family members in all combinations. We are expected to become friends with each picture.

Her husband, who is missing both his thumbs, puts on his cap and disappears to fetch the old man, who is still at work. After a while he brings him in, a sturdy man with a mustache: he makes me think of pictures of old Georgian men; will he get to be 120 as well? He deserves to.

The couple's young son, his grandson William, slender and dark, comes into the house, so now we have a short visit with the whole family. Even the boy speaks broken English, or does it just sound that way?

The whole family walks with us across a few fields, asking us quite formally to come again, even me, the foreigner, and everyone waves a long time.

Before dinner, Megan, the wife, shows us the "Chapel." It is on the farm, a few meters from the house, which dates from the fourteenth century. The chapel is simple and plain, a tablet on the wall, dedicated to Megan's great-grandfather, who was the minister here:

Born 1805
Born again 1825
Died 1849

Just behind the chapel, a little churchyard, almost all the headstones slate. The immediate and extended family have been buried here for a hundred years.

So the farm contains everything: the living, the animals, the chapel, the dead; and the old language is spoken always.

Your actual affection for people overcomes you when they are no longer around.

How scrupulously the participants in his seminar dissociate themselves from Kierkegaard! As if that were necessary for such zeroes!

Structures bore me; they are foisted upon us.

I spent many hours listening to people speaking in Wales. All I understood was a name now and then. While with them, I was happy (I often feel confined with people whom I understand). The enormous latitude for conjecture in the field of a completely foreign language. False interpretations, errors, nonsense thoughts. But also expectations, overestimations, promise.

Foreign languages as oracles.

People I haven't seen for a long time: I forget that they have died.

Imagine you are living back in your grandparents' day and have thought up everything to do with life today, without knowing it yourself.

Animals: we are more dependent on them than they on us: they our history, we their death. When they no longer exist, we will invent them all with effort out of ourselves.

Strike: Everyone decides never to leave their houses again. From this moment on, no door, no window is ever opened.

That is how they were found, three thousand years later, intact skeletons in intact houses, the only civilization that was ever known completely.

The bull bowed down before the matador and turned its back on the red cape.

He granted the bull its life and was torn to pieces by the mob.

He regrets nothing. He regrets everything. He regrets being seen doing so.

You are almost like the English; you always use the same words. But they are yours.

Don't say it's too late: how can you know you don't still have thirty years to begin a new life? Don't say it's too early: how can you know that you won't be dead in a month and that other people won't fashion lives for themselves out of the ruins of yours?

If I were made of steel, it would provoke her. I am made of words.

Whoever speaks with himself day after day, over and over again, is impressive: the power of journals.

Poems in alien surroundings have more effect on me. In inappropriate surroundings they affect me the most, for only there are they totally *isolated*.

I have to see many people to be alone, and it's important that I mean nothing to them.

When I dislike people, I get gruff and tough. In the presence of those I love I am nothing. Every effect I have on others transforms me into a fool.

At peace with everyone whom we have escaped.

The sycophant tries with every means to conceal how much he values the scrap that has fallen to him.

How can it be that you are so struck by the *tone* of the Bible, whose God revolts you so completely? It is only about him. For without God, the Bible would not strike your heart so.

It must be grief for God that strikes you, sorrow for the tough, stubborn, passionate attempt to create and keep alive a creator who will bear the responsibility for our unhappiness.

For it is unbearable to think that this senseless chaos is folded up, straightened out, and ruled by no one.

The folds, the order, the rules: the Bible's business.

A strong passion is useful in that it compels people to outwit it at the same time as they get to know it in its every detail.

He stood before his deadest departed, saying, "God is good." He repeated it over and over, a thousand, a hundred thousand times, but it did not raise the dead.

He still says God is good, but now the dead don't even return to him in dreams.

In the mouth of a young Jesuit priest I found God irritating partly because I did not know how how to react. But I found him particularly boring. I like reading about other gods; indeed, stories of gods interest me more than any others, but I avoid our God when I can. Yesterday the young Jesuit suddenly brought him into my room; the place felt strange to me, and I asked myself, "Where am I?"

The same evening the young Jesuit wrote to thank me. His letter was respectful, polite, and cordial. If only I knew whether letters like this are part of his discipline, arising out of missionary zeal, or whether he simply means what he says.

Through a kind of scientific discussion, in which certain names were mentioned and certain books produced, he and I established an immediate rapport. But then, before I could find out what I actually wanted to know (his daily routine), God came between us, and the young Jesuit eagerly, a bit rashly, wrapped himself in him. With this he lost all interest for me; he was transformed before my eyes into a child, a child of God, and of all human phenomena on earth, this is the one thing that bores me to distraction.

I am ashamed for people who fall for God. They are often good people. To be good themselves, these people need to have a power that names and describes goodness. To conquer their innate sinfulness, as we all try to do our own, they require obedience and prescribed exercises. They would be right were it not clear that their obedience has the character of all obedience, and since they do not understand this, they are working in the dark, transforming themselves, with enormous self-discipline, into *tools*.

But I have observed the tools of obedience and seen how they work. Total devotion has merit, but it must be balanced by an inborn *freedom*, and it is just this freedom that God cannot allow.

And so I listened to my youthful visitor's prattle, trying not to let him see that my displeasure was with the very core of his being.

But he was also curious, in his disciplined way. He listened carefully to what I had to say and tried to translate it into categories and patterns familiar to him. I noticed how my statements, which I had already softened and made less pointed, were transformed into something quite different. It was an unpleasant process. I even condescended to speak of the "absolute," in explaining why I would never give a name to anything that was truly unknown. But since I had said the word "absolute"—which I normally never do—anything else I could add was necessarily worthless.

Read two consecutive sentences of Kafka and you feel smaller than you ever have before. Kafka's passion for making himself insignificant is transmitted to the reader.

The story of the man who finds women to whom he delegates all the activities that he has taken upon himself to do. I call him the *slaveholder*. He is a nice, friendly man, but what happens to *them* is that they become so swollen with all his tasks that they burst.

Asking too many questions is death to a person who feels.

The discoverer, failing now, cursed by his wife, the only one who can still bear him. But even she can no longer bear him—she carries him.

A person who invents orders to give himself so as to avoid any from others. He amasses more and more orders, conducts his affairs, lives his life according to them, until he finally thinks of nothing but them and *suffocates*.

What can we do with the people from our pasts, with all those we have known? They keep turning up, more and more of them, a kind of transmigration, not of souls but of faces and not in the hereafter but *here*. Years ago I was so astounded by their turning up in totally new places, with different ages, jobs, languages, that I was determined to *write down* every occurrence of this phenomenon. But I did so only rarely, and they have gotten more and more numerous. Now they are proliferating so fast that I could never record them all.

What is it about these constantly recurring people? Is there really only a limited number of possible faces? Or can our memories be organized only with the help of such resemblances?

It is of no help at all to know that a solution does not exist for the only problem that does.

The fate of the man who hated the idea of surviving: he made sure that *he* was survived.

Clarity, but not at the expense of life, whose end is unclear. For it would not be better if we knew that it had a destination?

It goes against my grain to see anything about the "end." I need infinite openness and a life that doesn't simply seem like food for worms.

The laughter of asses and that of tigers.

In the strongest passions, those that make life worth living, there is no mercy.

But his love is so great that he includes even the hope of such mercy in it. Though seeing, he is blind.

A man decides to build himself a *Pantheon of the Forgotten*.

He wishes to change the names that make up our tradition. He believes all revolutions run aground on their sacred names. In his view, we need not the revaluation of all values but the replacing of all names. He thinks humanity must first go through a stage of being orphaned, until those names that he would put in place of the prior ones are strong enough to stand on their own.

He starts by repudiating the great writers, who have

(117)

been our staple diet for too long, and puts others in their place who are long forgotten.

He hunts for vanished religions and in their founders finds treasure: a new morality.

For him the great monuments of history—the pyramids, temples, and cathedrals—are no more than Augean stables.

The images of gods and idols are likewise hateful to him. He is his own archaeologist doing his own excavations. He finds *his* flowers in junk rooms and dunghills.

For him, the ancient languages that our modern ones feed on are not the most beautiful. Along the byways of history he finds other, better languages.

He shatters the dominant myths, whose misuse extends even into science, in favor of ones whose power remains unutilized.

He sees in laziness the dominant leitmotiv of history. Progress is made on crutches; we rely on the past rather than push its failed ideas away and proceed at our own pace.

But even the forgotten names, which he has substituted for the overly famous, are of use to him only as long as they are weak. As soon as they have established themselves, they are to be mercilessly removed.

To be sure, he has the young for himself, but he despises them for growing old.

He doesn't care about other people's appearance or about his own. He speaks in words, certainly, but doesn't overvalue them. He is well aware of their unforeseeable, dangerous burden. He lives without caring how he lives, so he lives well.

He has followers, like everyone else with conviction, but these in particular he keeps at arm's length.

He treats flatterers like lepers, faultfinders like friends, and grumblers like siblings.

He cannot remember even his family. His name is so unimportant to him that he does not change it.

He goes everywhere and talks to everyone. He refuses to meet with people a second time, because they have already spoken with him once.

He succeeds in recognizing no one; thus, he can be just. He doesn't always understand himself, but he is always understood. "You said . . ." "I said nothing." "But is that all you know?" "I know nothing."

The power of this "nothing" is greater than the "something" of others, only this power *is* something.

He keeps no appointments and never goes to the same place twice. He regards cities, especially the great, famous ones, as random places. Rome means as little to him as London, Paris as much as New York. On pictures he always gives things the wrong names. He calls Fujiyama Mont Blanc, and Lugano Leicester. The confidence he radiates is that of impartiality. He considers nothing beautiful that once was thought to be so. In the papers the first thing he notices is destruction, but because he doesn't approve of it, it keeps him free.

As soon as they attain power, how well they all get along. As for the others, it's as if they did not exist.

"Rather, the wise teacher is one who makes demands of his pupil in such a way that he keeps his character flaws veiled, hidden, and secret."

Ibn Zafar, 1169

The bungler who always gets what he does not want.

He still takes it seriously, that overused word whose hide was so scalded that it fell off long ago, never to grow back.

In the coarsest words I use to say it, the gentlest words lie hidden, untouchable.

An enemy you have to lend teeth to.

Fame is cursed when it makes a city *one* man's.

He sees with painful clarity that what he brought on himself will be his fate. At least he chooses to believe that he wanted what now must come.

It could be that writers who love death can never summon up the combative toughness that the hatred of death provides. Since they have no objection to death, they become spiritually flabby. Death doesn't trouble them, so nothing compels them to represent death in their work.

Now, there are writers who *appear* to accept death, so as to trick it, like Schopenhauer. In their inmost selves they remain deeply opposed to it, and this is betrayed in the way they write.

Pause after pause, and in between, quadrangles of words like fortresses.

He is proud that within him there is such a ferment of activity that future generations will never ossify in him.

All the people of the world, all the young people, came to Hampstead to see him.

Only those who can be bothered live. If you can't be bothered, you have already died.

Someday the prophets will realize that they see only into the past.

Nothing is so *antiquated* as power. Even faith is more modern.

I have read all the myths and sagas, avoiding those of the Jews. For twelve years the volumes have been standing by the door in my home. I have walked right by them every day, never thinking to open them. Have I had contempt for them? Have I feared them? I don't think it has been contempt. I am afraid of everything Jewish, afraid of falling under its sway. The well-known names, the age-old destiny, the Jewish way of questioning and answering gets into the very marrow of my being. But how can I be open to everything else if I become too absorbed with that which I already am?

I have been living in these sagas for the past few days and cannot get enough of them. I force myself not to read more than a hundred pages a day. If I had my way, I would do nothing else night and day but read and reread them one by one until I knew the contents of all five volumes by heart. I love the variations on a single story, elaborating what is really always the same. What I have found is the closest thing to Kafka—he has written the sequels to these stories. But they are also my stories; in every exaggeration I recognize my own spirit. I prefer the God of these stories to the one in the Bible—less of a zealot, more human, with a great deal of talk about animals. The animals in the Bible come off badly. But the best thing is the variations on identical themes, as if the tradition contained multiple meanings, with all the interpretations arrayed alongside one another, of equal worth. The moral, pervading everything absolutely, commands our respect. It is never shallow, never sounds preachy. It is both lesson and enlightenment. We feel ourselves in the company of a few sage men, thinking men who wish to be just, and I have been looking for such men my whole life. I have found just one, Sonne, and so everything I read here sounds as if it came from him.

As Adam still lay on the ground, a lump of clay, God pondered: "Shall I leave him thus?" He was pleased with the well-formed shape. If it breathed would it do evil? "Perhaps he does not deserve my giving breath to him?" For God was not omniscient; all that he created was independent of him. Nothing was predetermined, and all things came the way they wished. There was not even a louse that didn't crawl as it liked. And even the gazelle outran the lion when it cared enough to do so. For God had never imagined ruling over Creation. He would work his will and make things with it, and when they came to life and ran off, that was fine with him. Nor did he much want to remember all that he made. He wanted innovation: this and only this excited and amused him. God was alone, he was always alone, and all the stories about his companion are invention. One need only imagine what it was like to be alone. Would, say, a human have found it any easier? One comes upon all kinds of thoughts when alone, and these thoughts of God became Creation.

The excess fat in my works will turn rancid. Only a few sentences will remain. But which will they be?

The prophets deplore most deeply that which they themselves have brought to pass. How could they admit to themselves and grasp that their fears were justified?

The first truly human being would be one who never killed and never wished death for himself.

That the hubris of passion leads to madness: how can you revere the Greeks so if you did not learn that from them?

1967

The vilest letters he answers conscientiously. To serious ones he makes no reply at all. And why does he so carelessly squander the rare respect of their authors? He is totally fascinated by those who hate him. He counts his haters in every country and carefully decodes for himself what they have against him. How much he agrees with them! How much he understands them! They make him feel proud: how dangerous he is! He hears their words in seven dozen languages and translates them into his own. There are never enough: he is always hoping for more.

A man whom I had been avoiding used to go about on three words. The fourth was gone, but he enjoyed limping. He got around better than if he were whole. Sometimes he would sit at the roadside mending and cleaning things. If one of his words gave him trouble, he put it in his mouth. Once a dog bit him in his best word, but its rabies did no harm; the other two words were afraid, though. This is the state I found him in. I heard a word foaming at the mouth and stopped in my tracks, and soon this wreck was at my side. The owner politely asked me for help. I took it on my shoulder and couldn't get rid of it again. Now I am carrying the three words that carry him—I hear them whining for alms.

The believer guards his mistrust so as not to drown in happiness.

He is itching to mix sentences together till none means a thing.

He makes order for two months and then produces two sentences. In chaos, sentences feel poisonous.

He does not believe he will ever go silent. He puts his faith in the turbulent passion of words.

To sift one language through another: the sense and non-sense of translation.

Grieving for what is lost, as if we had destroyed it ourselves.

He was so good that no one ever remembered his name.

She kills every man who won't love her. But she also kills every man who does.

"Nothing pleases me more than presenting a totally false picture of myself to those people I have taken into my heart. Perhaps this is unfair, but it is daring and, so, correct."

Robert Walser, Jakob von Gunten

Those who maintain their simplicity while avoiding mere cleverness will find justification in the eyes of history. Those who cultivate their cleverness till they attain all that is due to the simple, posterity will view as scum.

A person wounds himself to see blood flow. A person kills himself to kill.

All those who despise him because he has never killed anyone. D. was of the opinion that only someone who has killed another is human.

The gap between the priestly castes and the castes of warriors and killers was certainly enormous, by its very nature. But these same priests still killed animals for sacrifices.

Are there not dreadful forces at work even in those who could never kill under any circumstances, forces that could gradually kill those nearest them?

Should we not have *one* completely false relationship in our lives, to make the other ones true and genuine?

He wraps everything he does inside something he has never done.

The parasite's problem: the life of his host, and thus his own, is threatened. He does not know what would be best for him. Has he stored up enough to start his own career, free of the host's control? Should he not store up more as fast as possible? Should he do everything possible to keep his host alive a little longer? Shouldn't he at least be present when the host dies, to give the report of the "sole survivor"? Since the threat, he panics if people stop seeing him for a while. He makes calls daily, but no one answers. Will he eventually have the courage to lie in wait outside someone's house, "out of concern"? He feels no gratitude; who is grateful for subsistence? He feels only resentment toward a subsistence that is suddenly being taken away.

So I have been living among the English for thirty years without knowing the nastier types among them. This fact does an injustice to the Viennese, among whom I knew just this type especially well.

The evil eyes attach themselves to God's wounds and are happy.

The man who does not live to see the murders of the future: how he hates his contemporaries!

He delves back into the centuries, retrieving that which they would rather have forgotten.

People were trained in special schools to dwell in the cities of old. There were Venetians, Toledans, Pompeians, Parisians. They walked about in period costumes and ate and drank only what was appropriate. They lived in their little dollhouses and were watched night and day. They had been told to act as though they were not aware of being watched. In the pubs they drank with gusto in front of a crowd of tourists. They were permanent employees, not allowed to take tips. They intermarried and produced children, but these were later taken from them. In the Sorbonne the students held debates in Latin; there were even goliards. The *attrapes* of Montmartre were very popular in Paris. In Venice the women bought theater tickets while masked, and the Biennale, as always, was just round the corner from Tintoretto. In Toledo, El Greco's house was balanced on real swords. In Pompeii those who had suffocated lay in every other house, some in the street, obscene epithets still on their lips. Everything was real, and visitors came by the millions.

She loved taking leave of other men right in front of her jealous lover. He never came upon her unless she was saying good-bye to someone else. It happened quite easily, as in a dream, but always right in front of him. Whenever he had a date with her, she was sitting with someone else. She got up as soon as he appeared, without saying good-bye to the other man. He never found her with the same man twice. She loved the activity of taking leave; he could have whistled to her and she would have come. He made sure that they were always alone when they parted. At particularly jealous moments he imagined seeing the other man face to face, the one who was waiting for her now. So long as this did not happen, he thought of himself as her true lover and remained faithful.

What if God had retreated from Creation, ashamed of having created death?

They compared her to a panther, but she hissed too late.

He said "we" when he meant "I." But in return he always said "I" for "you."

We do not spare ourselves; we want to experience everything that could hurt. We dig the deepest where we are most sensitive. What nonsense to think it is a love of pain that makes us do it. It is nothing but fear, fear of the transitoriness of the intensest, purest feeling. We seek destruction from the beginning, because it is waiting for us at the end.

Nothing is more boring than self-recrimination. It is pleasurable, but only when we know ourselves well and find an allowable target for this murderous harshness. Others do not and cannot know what we are talking about; they shrug and say, "What of it?" This is basically just another form of self-inflation. We find our own company more interesting if we can ascribe sinfulness to ourselves; complacency hides behind severity.

Someone is walking, constantly. He walks and walks. He never gets anyplace but keeps on walking. Occasionally he carries a stick but then loses it and goes on without it. He lets himself be seen walking. He sleeps walking. He dreams he is at rest, but he is ashamed of this, and no dream yet has caused him to stop in reality. He eats walking, pisses walking, takes advantage of any opportunity. Women admire him as they admire all men for something, and when a woman wants him badly, she figures a way to be loved by him walking. Some will even walk alongside him awhile, perhaps hoping to persuade him to come home with them. They soon give up; he is unalterably alone and won't let himself be disturbed again so easily. What does he think about while walking? He does not know—certainly thinking is not the main thing. He washes when going through water, drying off quickly in the wind. Does he notice every place he has been? Does he avoid the same places?

To surround oneself with people in the summer—no war and everyone is alive.

A summer in which not one person died.

The happy man, piqued by vanity. Now he wants to read and be unhappy.

Burn your old clothes, discard those phrases. No more defenses—leave the old and find what you are now.

The interesting thing about philosophies is their sense-lessness. They present us with various possibilities of the world. We need not choose any of them, but they need to exist. To be content to prove them all nonsense would be a silly game. For their nonsense is the most important, one might say the most vital, thing about them.

But in reality there is much more "marrow" to be extracted from religions.

The spirit in a cocoon but out there in the world, in all its din and discord, with one requirement: we must hold firm in our own din and discord and say nothing, not a word. If everything we hear cries out for an answer, *be silent.*

He who believed in a life hereafter reawakened the dead to *this* life. That is what comes to mind when I think about him; the rest is all a legend to me, but this, this for me is true.

The fog—she said this eight years ago—you will have to find the fog again so you can write. Then she disappeared in the fog herself.

He wants to be so successful that everyone loves him, and avoids him.

Is it good to *see ahead*? Can anything be averted by seeing ahead? Many people think that foreseeing something makes it come true. Others trust in free choice, *opposing* that which is foreseen. I act as if I believed both. Thus, I am bound and free at the same time. In this way, at high personal cost, I can fantasize that I know more about people, when in truth I am just floating in a void.

He would like to be made of fog, so no one could find him.

Seeing his beloved while hearing her suitors, he conveys to her their every word.

And so they file past, the young, proud and confident and less false; but without hypocrisy, they're nothing.

"Man *is* pity and fear. There is nothing else."

Cesare Pavese

There is hearing, reading, recording. But can we say this to pity, to fear?

Today read only in Hebbel's journal.
I still find it a wonderful book. As chance would have it, last week I picked up Lichtenberg. I am closer to him than to Hebbel, which may be because what Lichtenberg

writes is closer to my idea of a sketch, while what Hebbel writes is a diary studded with random ideas. The running account of his rise as a writer occasionally bothers me—there is something self-satisfied about it. Lichtenberg has the advantage of being unbiased while Hebbel is heavier, often gloomy. Lichtenberg's ideas are purer; they exist for their own sake. Hebbel always has a motivation: perhaps he could do something with them. I am powerfully drawn to Lichtenberg's lavishness; Hebbel is more economical. Still, I don't know of any journals in German that mean more to me.

While reading Hebbel's journal: how little one has written oneself! And one really doesn't notice that Hebbel, too, left most things out. How rich his years seem, summed up.

Phrases that shy away from one another.

Faces only decipherable two thousand years later.

A hide made of tiny mollusks.

He eats while sleeping, he eats when making love; walking, lying, kneeling, speaking, weeping, groaning, dying, he eats.

"The sleeping calf, rescued from the butcher's cart."
Hebbel, Journals *(age twenty-three)*

A. says the older we get, the more we sense that there are no *other* geniuses.

An infinity of figures, all unused; he'll touch them only after they've been forgotten.

The blind man gives his eyes to another, who *sees with them.*

A brain as hard as a cobblestone, hurled at doubt.

He would like to be swimming in money so he could throw it after everyone he despises.

The world's esteem is quite worthless unless we despise it. But how can we think of despising it when we eke out our life with it? So then there is just one way out: to be rich, and that is no way out because it takes too much from us.

Today I denied myself Robert Walser for fear he would become a kind of narcotic.

Acquittal via self-recrimination.

Gnawing on his uniqueness, he wasted away and died of starvation.

He babbles blood and exudes epistles.

I need a lot of foreigners around me, and the heavens dump them down here in Hampstead like a cloudburst.

He fails at arrivals but is a master of departure.

This tendency of the successful to praise one another. As if they were then more what they want to be, since even their rivals confirm it for them. But it is a fact that a contemporary's praise is no help, because it is never disinterested. "Say something good about me, and I will say it about you."

So it is a truly awkward situation when we come across someone we really admire and suddenly notice how highly he himself has always regarded us.

Most important: to forget what one has made. But to do this one must have made something too.

Today the legitimation of a work is the evil in it, and in this age the idyll has died forever. The arena of life is varied, and its monstrous tension is our daily trial.

Having no peace, we must listen in God's stead and burst from doing so. No one is good enough and open enough for sainthood in this century, with its sacrificial madness, and its martyrs cannot know *for what* they were martyred.

A heaven, in despair of mankind, arching itself ever farther away.

He always says the same thing, but each time it becomes one sentence longer. Since he says it so often, it swells to monstrous size, and finally there is no time left intervening for him to be silent.

Look for someone to make you *slow*.

Phrases like eyelashes.

A half tree held the street upright.

The English expression "I appreciate": embarrassing. Its tone a mixture of "pressure" and "price," as if one wanted to say, "I will keep pressing till the price is right." But without the pressure, the price wouldn't mean anything. One of the arrogant expressions of the English language—in this, the language is inimitable.

The dog barks the riot act at him.

A woman dies of a disease that is incurable; her lover is in despair. Soon after, he contracts the same disease. Meanwhile a cure for it is discovered, and *he* recovers.

That monstrous heart in which the cities settle.

To find a person who has never yet told the truth—and no one has ever noticed.

A person he likes so much, it's as though in an earlier life he had *escaped* from him.

We need only say, "Years, years," and the hasty drop to their knees.

Everything you don't like in others is really what you don't like in yourself, and knowing this, you are a *broken* satirist, one whose black wings have been clipped.

The monologue has become so insipid, vacuous, sterile, boring, wordy, tasteless, colorless, odorless, it would be better to talk to someone, *anyone*. This person could even be invented, just so long as "I" and "you" finally disappeared, rotted away, evaporated.

He, he, he, just *he,* something of the timidity and chasteness of Kafka instead of loudmouth confessional posing.

Yesterday R.T., the poet who was long crippled, proudly showed off her *real* fingernails.

There couples embrace each other so long that they become grafted together. Then the couples must embrace other couples, until they also graft together.

He found it pleasant to torture his dog at home and then take him for a nice walk.

It would be more to your liking if you had another word for myth: there is none.

I take immense pleasure from people who come here from afar, especially the young, as if they could make the earth's condition more *elastic*.

Poets are unbearable to one another. You have to see them with other people to know what they're like.

"Supply of Faces": sometimes the storehoused faces can't stand being kept in the dark and fling themselves upon actual human beings, whom they then appropriate by force.

Aristophanes: *The Peace*

The dung beetle as Trygaeus's mount; slaves feeding him dung at the beginning. Trygaeus's fear of manure smells on earth during his ascension to Zeus.

This first stink-filled idea is strong and unforgettable.

The scene where they string rope about the buried goddess of peace is much weaker.

The rest of the play is a panegyric to the joys of peaceful life, and in this it is true, natural, and relevant for every age from then to now, the sigh of the simple man after every war. But the comic sections within, for example, when the victors enter, are not Aristophanes' best. As is often the case with him, individual objects (helmet, armor, etc.) have odd significance.

House pet: A fat queen termite.

The poet who invented the language of the bees, and it is spoken.

The biggest hypocrite may write about the most honest: literary history.

Some believe they can pass as mystics by saying, "One! One! One!" Others try through fragmentation, by doing everything in their power never to be "one."

Enemies, so that they can be talked into friendship.

The blind man announces what he *would* have seen.

The man who also *knows* all the animals he is.

How fortifying rejection is! So critics, whose whole enterprise consists of it, may easily seem to themselves like supermen.

He reads the satirists, too, to know what hate is. In Aristophanes, in Quevedo, in Swift, he understands his own hatred.

It must be very funny, his speaking about immortality. And yet that is what he really wants, and wants not just for himself *but for everyone he has known.*

A sleep so long that we awake to just a dream. But then, in this dream, a full life.

The concentration I seek tears my breath apart.

Amazing about satirists, that they can spare *themselves* so long. Not all of them become idiots; many grow old. Gogol alone destroys himself early—is this why, among those we know most about, he is the greatest?

In order not to forget time, he lives only where it *whirs*.

"Ce que j'aime du voyage, c'est *l'étonnement au retour*."
Stendhal

Once again, as in the last war, news of natural catastrophes not caused by human action is somehow comforting. Can anything more horrible be said about the condition of our world?

Marvelous, the conversations we don't have.

When someone says "gods," he is saying that besides the god that now inhabits him there is something else, a lot else, no less worthy of being divine. Thus, for the world a single god is not all-embracing or all-destroying. And so other gods can set themselves up against this one god, revitalizing and extending the shrinking world.

There are ideas so revolting that we can never get rid of them. It appears that the power of many great writers consists in just this.

Yesterday Plato's *Symposium*—I had not read it for a long time. What touched me most was the speech of Aristophanes, as grotesquely inventive as if written by himself, and that of Alcibiades at the end, the eulogy for Socrates. In this latter presentation—clear, immediate, and inspired by passionate admiration—Socrates is a tangible object of love. It is unutterably beautiful how the discussion of love is itself crowned and completed by actual love. Alcibiades' devotion to Socrates creates a perfect picture of him, and could there be anyone who would not want to be like *that* Socrates?

Socrates' *method*, the thing about him that I have always abhorred—his quibbling sophistry—recedes into the background in the *Symposium*. There is enough of it present to make one feel glad that there is less than usual. And anyway, it has to do with his discourse on "what men most want," on immortality. Socrates' claim, which elsewhere often gets unbearable—his "moral," so to speak— that man desires good makes it look as if he is "covering" himself: in reality it is he, Socrates, who wants the good, and how much trouble he takes to persuade other men that *they* desire it! He is the daimon of good, and it should not be forgotten that Plato wrote the *Symposium after* Socrates was publicly sentenced to death and poisoned. His end is tragic, and it is Alcibiades—the person most responsible for his death, whose actions weighed most heavily in the balance against him—who delivers the encomium for him. There is something charming about the drunkenness that moves him to speak openly. Right at the end, after all the others have left the dinner or fallen asleep, Socrates continues his discussion with Agathon and Aristophanes, the tragic poet and the comic poet, trying to prove to them that the two figures are really *one* and belong together.

Can one who reads only Plato become a poet?

The question, the fearful question: whether men really change.

In the *Symposium* Plato says yes, as if he had just read Heraclitus. They bear the same name for a lifetime, he says, but are different—everything about them and in them is always different.

I do not trust this assessment; I am not at all sure of it. I know where I am the same as I always was. It is hard for us to see where we are different.

God crawled into his ear, and how much he hears!

The blind man recognized him, and he felt very flattered.

He had a lover whom he visited only after funerals. She liked him then. "You are so different after funerals," she would say to him, "you love me more passionately. I don't like you any other way." She would read the obituaries for him and notify him by phone when she thought he should go. Right off, she would say, "Do you know who died?" Sometimes he wouldn't have heard from her for three or four weeks. "Who?" "N.N. You knew him. You'd better go." "What time?" "Monday at three in the crematorium. I'll expect you then." She would immediately feel better when she had found a funeral for him and would get everything ready for his visit. He went, saw, and heard for himself, and he actually liked going, because he knew what was coming next. But he was not a cynic, or else the funerals would not have upset him. He thought about the deceased, he pictured him or her to himself, carried on old conversations with the person. The dead got to him so much that without cheering up he could scarcely have gone on living. Bent and aged, he would start off for her house. She would be standing behind the curtain and would see him on the street. Throwing the door open, she would say, "Welcome!" She would always wear something that reminded him of the special occasion, something small and quite discreet, but he always noticed it gratefully.

"Come," she would say, "you are exhausted. It's really taken a lot out of you." He would nod, come in, and sit down, a bit timidly, in the best chair. She would sit near him but maintain a certain distance. "Tell me! Was it very bad? Maybe you'd rather not talk about it." "Not for a while," he would say—it seemed better that way. After all, he was no monster, he had feelings, he had to take a little breather before admitting to himself that life would go on. "Don't take it to heart so," she would say, with tears in her eyes: she was suffering with him. He was grateful for every move that demonstrated her understanding and concern. "Did it take a long time?" she would ask then. "Not especially. Luckily it was short. I don't like ceremony. It's such a terribly difficult thing in any case. You think you'll break down if it doesn't stop soon." "How was the minister?" "Not bad. Quite short and sweet. Afterwards he stood by the door and shook everyone's hand. I always wonder whether to give him something." "But you can't do that." "He has this way of holding out his hand. I think he could hide it well enough that nobody would notice." "Were there a lot of flowers?" "Mountains, but not as many as last time." "Must be beautiful, all those flowers." "Sometimes there are none, by request." "Yes, I remember. Time before last when you were here there were no flowers." "You have a good memory." "I live only for you. I share all your troubles with you." "That's true. I just don't know how I could go to funerals without you." "I hope you never do." "How could I deceive you?" "Sometimes I think you were someplace without telling me." "But you read all the notices. You don't miss a single one." "I'm not infallible. If I don't see you for six weeks, I think I must have missed something." "Hopefully you read more than one paper." "Sure, of course, but there are people who don't put a notice in the paper." "Then I wouldn't know about it either." "Do you get any private notices at home?" "I throw out anything with a black border. I leave everything up to you. Without you I'd be lost." After this little jealous scene, which he is used to and which only follows funerals, he puts out his right hand and clasps her knee.

A friend who's made of news.

Your ear is older than your grandfather.

Hausa saying

1968

A man was standing there saying: *That's all!* He said it at regular intervals, probably afraid to say anything else, and though full to bursting with phrases, he held back, simply repeating: *That's all!* It is possible he was directing this exclamation at himself, but then he would have been less loud, and bystanders and pedestrians interpreted him differently: they thought he meant *them*. He stood there stiffly, but still very angrily, and kept repeating, without a letup, *That's all!* Was everyone walking supposed to stop, and everyone just standing supposed to get moving? Were those speaking meant to go silent, the silent to start speaking? Or did his command have a more general meaning: was life itself now supposed to come to an end? He was committed to some change, everyone felt that, and though only a few people obeyed, his command stuck in the minds of everyone, whether nearby or some distance away; everyone heard it as bad news and felt depressed.

Maybe the man's shouting was an attempt to unload his burden onto as many others as possible. A prophet so severe that the religion he was founding consisted of this one inescapable phrase.

A great many ideas want to remain comets.

He talked himself blind.

When she is scurrying about me, all my unlived days are illuminated.

Whoever is not corrupted by names is charmed: *his word shall prevail.*

All the thinkers there have their heads shaved, as a warning. No one goes anywhere near them. Any contact with a thinker is considered a great misfortune.

And the shaven-headed themselves avoid one another. They, too, believe the common superstition. They live alone in little plague huts. But their hair brings good luck, and people fight over it.

There was just a single story by him, which he republished every ten years. As his fame grew, this story seemed more and more interesting. It was never recognized by anyone who had read it before. A thousand essays and a hundred books appeared to interpret it. It was talked about everywhere, and he was accorded the honors befitting a demigod. He was the writer everyone knew.

When I think of Kafka, I feel like Grimmelshausen's Springinsfeld or like a student, sometimes the one, sometimes the other, but never anything more, and I must admit to myself that I am too crude ever to be wise.

The tone that pervades Kafka: like weakness as a sound. But it isn't weakness, it's a renouncing of the beyond; what remains is the sound of that renunciation.

Your inflated praise has destroyed her tenderness. Now she needs your praise as she would a narcotic and grasps for it even in dreams.

Wise the man who never mastered gluttony.

When he got home, all the windows of his house had turned to doors, and in every one stood one of his enemies.

Everyone there is sentenced to temporary blindness. To three, five, ten years of blindness. But knowing they will then see again.

A good man asked me the way. "I dare not tell you," was my answer. He looked at me, friendly, if astonished. But he said nothing and seemed satisfied with my reply. He continued uncertainly, and from the way he walked it was evident that he would not be asking anyone else. Sadly I looked after him. Should I have told him the truth? I knew that he had to die; death was waiting for him on any road I might have pointed to. If he had known, he might have stood still, and this was all that could save him: standing still.

"Stay right there," I called after him. He heard me, but since I had dismissed him, he dared not stop but kept going. "Stop!" I called, louder—he walked faster. Then, tortured with guilt, I shouted it, and he started running.

A compliment that takes years to catch.

He has broken Kafka on his neat little wheel.

On this point the spirits disagreed: were they better off yesterday, or will they be tomorrow?

Everything is bearable. Unbearable only is an attack on the people whom we love more than all else. Extrapolate from this what the faithful must feel when we insult God.

My incessant self-abasement before Kafka:
    Because I am a careless eater? (I have never given what I eat a second thought.)
    Because he strives for a precision I cannot achieve? (I only know the precision of my exaggerations.)

Because I have shown I can experience happiness and not run from it?

Because I can communicate easily, unreservedly, and I feel how that would horrify him?

Because he did not leave a single hair of his head untouched by self-criticism? (I live under a dense pelt of healthy hair.)

Because, infected by him, I have merely traded in my own brand of self-hatred for his?

Words that are used only once in a lifetime. Which ones?

He's afraid his works might eat one another up, so he keeps them on a short lead.

Too old, too old! Now even the streets stand up for him.

To find our way to ourselves by noting what we have an aversion to.

There are dogs so lazy that they refuse even to sniff one another.

Brecht's lasting effect: proliferation of the word *listig* (subtle, sly, tricky).

Six days in Vienna make us false for six years.

He shows her images of eternity, confusing them with
her eternal salvation. She doesn't care a fig for them; she
prefers to devour his strength now.

Kafka: I grovel in the dust before him; Proust: my fulfillment; Musil: my intellectual exercise.

1969

On the whole it may be said that *less* is known today, now that there are droves of blinkered, jargon-spouting appointees to knowledge. What has been gained in the specific has been lost in the general.

That the behavior of dictators is perfidious is no longer surprising. But that mankind still craves authoritarianism, despite their appalling record of failure, is incomprehensible. With these monstrous examples right before our eyes, how are we so stupid, and how is it possible, faced with *all* that has happened, for us to lie to ourselves again and again?

When she is far away, she visits often. But once here, she takes her leave again.

In the Japanese city of Tsuretsuregusa there is record of a hermit who was not unwilling to depart this earth but *felt sorry about giving up the heavens*. (By this he meant the visible, earthly sky.)
    The most attractive thing about Japanese drawings is

(159)

their sensuousness. Even hermits see and breathe it and tell of it.

Great writers who disappeared because their pupils were more successful. Writers who disappeared because they were themselves too successful.

Writers who only exist because they became known so late.

If we know everything about someone, what is left of him? Just what we forget.

A god who could be any animal but never like a man.

The pre-traitor: a man who betrays secrets he has not yet been told.

He begins with the revelation of a secret that has yet to exist, so he has to create it after the fact. He deals in retroactive secrets, so to speak. The trick in all this is that eventually he has to persuade the people who supposedly entrusted him with the secrets to believe those secrets that he has already "revealed."

So in order to have any role at all, he has to conspire with those whom he wants to trick.

The question of time and who has sent him. He uses the money he receives for his pre-betrayals to make the secrets come true. (He could be thought of as a kind of poet, trying to influence reality to strengthen his inventions.)

He gives the impression of being quite experienced, for he makes up all the experiences himself. He never wears disguises. He is never interested in the outcome of his plots; he needs newer, bigger conspiracies and, in the end, is gladly brought down by their consequences.

The false builder who lures people into houses that he has constructed in such a way that once inside them the people wreak their own destruction.

The man who becomes *good* through the vanity of others.
It would be very important to find a way to make use of evil, so that one would get better and better from the baseness of others.

"Voluptas ex felicitate alieni"—Leibniz.
(Ecstasy from the happiness of another.)

I can only believe her if I believe her very much. I have to overdo it, go to nearly ridiculous lengths. I cannot just believe.

The memory wants to come undisturbed, in its own moment, and must not be bothered by anyone who was present then.

Perhaps the gods of old, in just that shrunken, starved form they had, could still be very useful as gods of poverty.

Now the planetarium has become a terrarium, and we cannot gaze upon the planets without feeling somewhat confined and oppressed by their attainability.

By our reaching for the planets, astrology itself will be proved right. As *our* colonies, they may well turn out to be our fate, though something different from astrology's claims. In any case, without it, the planets would never have been important enough to us.

Unfathomable the extent of the spoken word, as if the intention was once to persuade the whole world of something.

Find one abstemious man who has never said anything that was not necessary for survival.

I knew him back when he still recognized me. Now I have known him so long that he doesn't recognize me anymore.

He ran away from everybody until he learned to his astonishment that somebody ran away from him.

Find statements so simple they never can be one's own again.

Whatever he experiences quickly assumes the dimensions of a tree. Is this what we call *mythic* potential? Are these trees myths? Some of them or just one? Which ones? Are the leaves involved and what is the tree without them? Some use a different word, not *growth* but *exaggeration*. But the tree doesn't just grow up, it reaches out on all sides, winding and twisting and becoming one with its surroundings. What matters is its rampant growth, its luxuriance, and part of this is the confusion, combination, and interpenetration of all its components.

A guilt built on nothing but justifications, which alone keep it from resolving itself.

To get a more accurate picture of a new person, one should approach him in various disguises that he cannot see through. As oneself, in one's real persona, one forces limitations on him that one then holds against him.

How often one is quick to revive grudges against those one has injured. Sensing the injustice of what one is doing, one justifies it with a dormant grievance from the past.

People don't change at all, and they change enormously; it is completely confounding that both can be true at once.

The core of my nature is that I cannot humble myself but must transform myself nonetheless. I cannot look to death for my transformation. Therefore, with unwavering obstinacy I see death as the end.

I know that I have still said *nothing* about death. How long will I defer my final judgment? Or must I deny myself this, out of hatred for death?

Creatures made of one eye, rolling along.

The ship that never sinks: malice.

And in what place would you not suffocate? And what is the use of digging for the roots of things everywhere? Roots are all so awfully similar.

The chaotic way we depart the world, leaving people of all ages behind.

With nothing left to confess, he has no need of friends.

If there is one thing I never want to be, it is "timely." For any time should suit me. It is not I who should suit it, as I am not worthy of it—it could as well be another time, and anyone bringing it to me would be more than it, and I, I would be merely incidental to it.

Since he started saying *du* to himself, he hasn't got anything to say.

The impossibility of preserving what he knew. But it can be forgotten in such a way that it is transformed.

There are countless *things* the world is heading toward that can only fill one with the deepest disgust. But this is not enough: one has to think them through and fight them. Mankind, more and more the creator of this world, should say, "It is *not* good."

"Where do I find the man who forgets words, that I might converse with him?"

Chuang-tze

The man living outside the ordinary concepts of time. He never knows what day of the week it is. He knows neither month nor day, let alone year.

But he knows people and lives among them. How does he do it? He is removed from the passage of time; it does not register with him. Clocks are as foreign to him as calendars, and history does not exist for him.

He is a worthy counterpart to the man who constantly tries to get things at the lowest price. I have always considered this type a spendthrift. But isn't the man who lives without time also a kind of spendthrift? The mere fact of always having time differentiates him from everyone else:

perhaps his story should be called "The Man Who Always Has Time."

Chuang-tze contains both the very *small* and the very *large*. One half is like Kafka, but there's another half as well—thus, he's all the more complete.

Nowhere but in Confucius does there exist such a conscious and systematic depiction of models. Through him, the rulers of the ancient world (and there are any number of them) all partake of a certain similarity—basically they are *like him*.

That state of mind which was never quite credible in Aristotle is entirely so in Democritus.

The couples who need a new blessing. Where should they find it, and what blessing should it be? Is it the blessing of separation, since everything else is quite permissible? Do they need an "outward" distance since the "legal" one no longer exists? Would couples then have to be separated from each other right after they met? Would it be necessary for them to transform their distance into desire, which they would have to resist since it is, after all, irresistible?

What is the significance for them of letters and the telephone? Do these turn out to be the real locus of their love?

Probably it is impossible to live without goals. But to stay fresh in their pursuit, we learn to juggle. We toss them up into the air, doing whatever we must to catch them again. The balls, all confusingly similar, don't really matter; it is the movement that does.

An eye that twitches when it doesn't like what it sees.

New vehicles in which we move more slowly than we walk: salvation.

For every accusation an innocent party is carefully selected. The guilty are freed immediately, on principle.

Totally empty countries alternate with overcrowded ones. The empty ones have to stay empty.

A select few are chosen by lot to be fathers; no one but they may procreate.

Good deeds are forbidden, to make them more attractive.

After every "appearance" (if this was indeed necessary), a "spiritual" man would be required to desert his followers in such a manner that they could not find him again. If they did find him, he would have to disguise himself so they thought him someone else. If they were still able to unmask him, then he would have to make himself small, sickly, weak, just to get away. Far removed from them, protected from their impertinent adoration, he could slowly become himself again.

"Contamination" by opponents, one of the most effective political phenomena, not well enough understood.

Happy and in love now, he says "God" less frequently.

He puts words on and takes words off, letting language operate on its own, and thinks this striptease is Literature. Without ever having a thought of his own, he draws his wisdom from the common tap and is happy that everyone understands him straight off.

In a single night of reading he learned more about fleas than he had in the entire sixty-four years of his life. The concentration of the learnable. But twenty-five years earlier he found in Donne the most powerful love poem of the English language, called "The Flea." So should he now balance this Donnean flea against the plague?

A tightrope walker whose words no longer support him. To the right and left of them he tumbles to the floor. He increases their tension again, tries, and tumbles once more.

Perhaps it is this last creation of words that he has made, this huge, powerful love, that is the most dangerous. But at least it is bold and lives by its own resources. At least it consumes, without reserve or restraint, that which nourishes it. If he knew he would die of it tomorrow, he still could not take back any of it.

The curse of being a public person—the opinions and positions people expect of you! As if you had anything to say that had not already been said a thousand times better!

Not all our insights come to us naturally. Occasionally we unexpectedly come across one anew and are amazed to see we have already noted it in our work.

There are *stationary* insights, ones that we float past, as if they had been placed on the shore and we merely see them as we flow by them like a stream.

"Whoever feeds tigers should be careful not to give them living creatures, on account of their ferocity, which is aroused through killing. Care should be taken not to give them whole creatures, on account of the ferocity aroused by tearing them apart. Their hunger must be stilled in time to head off their ferocity."

Chuang-tze

Late fame is impotent, because it reveals itself to be accidental.

To enjoy fame requires innocence and stupidity. One has neither when fame arrives late.

A creature that, through its intake of food, expands to infinite size.

The speck of dirt that catches the light like a coin.

He has withdrawn from everything new and now lives off his own saliva.

The satisfaction of one who plays chess with his own assertions.

Collect all the things in your life you've avoided.

The most peaceful place on earth is among strangers. Alone, one has the most vivid conception of others, and thus one is least alone.

Now Africa has become—for how long?—the primal home of man. Patiently we await archaeological discoveries on the moon.

For a photograph of the entire world, of every type of people on earth, I would need another hundred years. So I'll have to content myself with the first straw fire of curiosity.

It's the *formulas* of other languages that we cannot master, at least not sufficiently for them to yield the wisdom submerged within them.

He selects for himself new languages to be silent in.

Malraux's conversations with "great" men like Corneille. His consciousness of "history." He believes in "the great"; he approves of them, wants them, seeks them, ingratiates himself with them: a journalist with a higher agenda.

The woman who offered her solicitude to the bushmen, bringing along her mother and brother so as not to frighten them, who took them into her family and as a result was taken into theirs: I record her name here and hope never to forget it:

Elizabeth Marshall Thomas of Boston.

After more than twenty-five years I am still an apprentice of the bushmen. More than I can learn from them I don't want to know. But I have not come very far in my knowledge of them, for atom bombs and moon voyagers disturb me and constantly interrupt my study.

Wonderful to arise half asleep, to sit at my desk half asleep, to write half asleep.

A country where you never see people eating. The secrecy of eating.

What in our land is just the secrecy of elimination, is there the secrecy of the entire process from beginning to end.

Everyone there has just the amount of space that fits under an umbrella. No one goes out without one, and everyone puts his up. No one comes too close to anyone else. A distance is preserved. There is freedom everywhere. When acquaintances meet, the umbrellas are made to bow. How dignified are these greetings from umbrella to umbrella.

Accusations increase one's illustriousness.

"A friend of mine": one of the greediest English expressions when *spoken*.

It sounds as if this friend were being denied to the person being addressed. The friend remains indefinite, unnamed; he is private property, protected. The only noticeable thing about him is that he is "mine." It is announced that he exists, but he is concealed, as if he were being kept behind one's back and one were about to use him for an ambush.

A man who remembers only words in new languages, and in the process, the old ones gradually crumble away. He is alive so long as sounds have new meanings for him. He has the optimism of new definitions and unheard-of accents. He has escaped the tyranny of the beaten path. So the way I spoke before was all wrong, he tells himself. At last I am really learning to speak.

1970

Nothing should be counted as cognition that has not caused us great torment. All other insights have a mathematical or technical character, and their consequences overtake us because we have not suffered in winning them.

The urge to say something a hundred times; the wish to keep it secret.

It is said that in a remote mountain valley of New Guinea men have been discovered who walk on all fours.

Their horror of those who walk erect—they regard them as a kind of bird and hunt them like birds of paradise.

How it pleases one phony when I tell him about another!

He would like to write his last works as if he had never heard a thing about modern literature. He would like to be as old-fashioned a writer for his day as Stendhal was for his.

Memoirs! Memoirs! Maybe one should read memoirs only? The memoirs of Herzen, which I am now reading, fascinate me such that my every thought, day and night, returns to them. I read them almost the way I read Dostoyevsky at twenty, three hundred pages at a sitting. All other reading soon loses its hold on me; I break off, leave it for days, but in this case it is hard for me to be interested in other things for even an hour. Now, it is true that I *began* with volume 3 of my edition, with Herzen's stay in London. So it is all familiar: the Germans, the English, the French, the Italians, and, from literature, even the Russians. My chief experience, emigration, is prefigured here: the emigration that lasts a lifetime.

This is intentional emigration, and for twenty years I, too, had the nucleus of my being here, an aim and a goal I could never let go of; in this I was as dogged and unwavering as Herzen. I was no less impressed than he by the institutions of the English, and the emigré world surrounding me during the war was even more colorful than his.

I feel a kinship with Herzen in many ways. His pessimism: he *sees through* people, and it is not only because they want so much from him that he sees them as they are. He finds them amusing—there is much of Gogol in him—and while most of his efforts fail, while he knows that for the most part they cannot succeed, he never gives up hope: in the end he is devoted to mankind. This is all the more remarkable in that he had to deal with the most horrible variety of all, *political* man.

A poet he is not, but he is still a close relative of those Russian poets without whom the world would be inconceivable. Herzen writes in defense of his money, which of course he needs for legitimate purposes. Nonetheless it is not easy to view this defense from the same perspective. I tell myself that I defend my autonomy, my loneliness, my need for solitude. In this I am just as stubborn as he in the defense of his wealth.

By drawing such dubious parallels as these, I try to overlook certain aspects of him that should not weigh too heavily in the balance, measured against his richness as a person.

He makes an unusual variety of personal observations—he is not fanatic. He sees people as complex and various and does not begrudge them their inconsistencies, despite strong moralistic convictions that sometimes border on bourgeois prejudices.

His repeated references to the London fog seem a bit banal, but he lived in the south a long time and it is a very black fog.

His various moves about London: he changed dwellings here frequently. Overrun as he was with company, perhaps he wanted now and again to surround himself with greater space.

I find it agreeable that human *autonomy* meant much to him, even when expressed in the restricted forms of English Victorianism. He makes one more sensitive to any form of slavery.

To me he seems a dyed-in-the-wool human being, and by that I mean someone who never forgets anyone, no matter who he is or what he meant to him. The fact that he cannot forgive the lazy or the degenerate is understandable in view of the circumstances in Russia that he was trying to change. The cosmopolitan life he led provided him with enough of the picturesque—unlike less sophisticated people he did not have to seek it in decadence. He was no believer in religion, so his rejection of power was not absolute; since he had political goals, there also had to be acceptable ways of exerting power. One cannot expect him to die for a cause.

His warmth and generosity seem too good to be true, and even in his fundamental attitudes the traces of his origins are always clear.

What I have said about him to this point is provisional and incomplete because I still know nothing at all of his early period in Russia.

Herzen's love for Leopardi. His quarrel with Mazzini, who couldn't stand Leopardi.

While living among emigrés Herzen got to know the national characteristics of all kinds of Europeans, who these days are even *more* so than then: *his* mankind of the future.

The young Austrian officers on the Lake Lugano steamer are reminiscent of the ones in Karl Kraus's *The Last Days of Mankind*.

I can't get away from Herzen. I am starting the first volume now, after having decided last night to take a break.

What is it that is more true about an autobiography than about any other kind of narrative?

That one doesn't get too far off the central topic? That the references are different, nearer, less impartial?

Or just that "I" is in fact "I," and "he" really is "he"?

True, invention can be more demanding, but somewhere it has to begin arbitrarily. This very arbitrariness is just not possible in an autobiography; it begins with birth, which does not depend on one at all. Since we know nothing about our births, we can begin only at a point that we do know something about, and that point has long been the same.

Invention's quality of surprise, its advantage, can also be arbitrary. Later, in the context of our own lives, this arbitrariness is no longer possible. We must stay with that which our best understanding tells us is the truth. This truth is what matters, and it is on its account that we set down our life in writing.

Herzen's uncle, his father's oldest brother:

"Though already retired, he followed in the newspapers the promotions of his former colleagues in the service and participated with them step-by-step in their advancement, buying the medals they received and laying them out on a table as a sad reminder of the decorations he himself would have received."

My heart leaps when I read Herzen. I have only now started to read about his youth and cannot understand why I began with the third volume (the English period), continued with the second (the revolutionary year 1848), and am just now at the beginning, his youth. I can think of only one reason for this totally cockeyed way of reading a book that so fascinates me. Since August 1968, since the Prague occupation, I cannot bear to read about things in Russia itself. Before that, in reading about the time of the serfs, I shared the hopes of those who were writing about it. Today, when I do the same thing, I sink into deep despair.

"Neither Danton nor Robespierre, nor even Louis XVI, lived past thirty-five."

Aleksandr Ivanovich Herzen

On death: "Vadim died in February 1843. I was present at his passing, and that was the first time I experienced the death of someone close to me. I experienced it all the more strongly for its unmitigated horror, its pointless randomness, and all its stupid, immoral injustice."

Herzen

The thunderstorm at dawn. I was right in the middle of it; the storm was inside the room, the ceiling cracking like thunder. It went into other houses on my street, missing none, then back to my house again, getting into the books, even closer than the lightning bolts striking to the left and right all round. Nonetheless it was a gentle storm, perhaps because it was so low, suited more to a mass of houses and rooms than to cliffs and mountains. And after the unbearable heat and humidity, it was a blessing.

"We hang at eight and breakfast at nine": invitation from the governor of Newgate.

It is not enough to say everything is death.

Of course everything is death.

But we must also say, no matter how hopeless it seems, that we will firmly and fiercely oppose the fact that everything is death. Deprived of tricks or illusions, death will lose its respectability. Death is false. Our intent is to prove it so.

People acting out of the conviction that there is nothing but death strengthen it.

Out of their hatred for death, some of the best writers of our time have become its eulogists—a residue of Christianity in them, a misleading remnant.

He wants to be brief, as though he might be recalled at any moment. He wants to be so deep that he can never again be recalled.

The simplicity of religions attracts me to them enormously, but to all of them.

Some people wanted to be forgotten and to disappear completely. Abraham Sonne was one of these, a man without fault, the only man whom I admired and loved without the least reservation.

Others who knew him earlier or later thought the same of him. But now we cannot leave him alone. The few poems he wrote, in Hebrew, have been printed. A young British Jew translated them into English. One quite splendid poem is about his deepest wish, to vanish and leave no trace of himself. Broch created his *Death of Vergil* from the conversations they had. I speak of him often; whenever I want to speak of people at their most wonderful, I speak of Sonne. I had conversations with him through four lean years in which *he* was the only substance, but I never wrote them down. Still they have become so much a part of me that they really are *my* substance; they are the most important ring of the tree I sometimes feel I am, a four-year ring. If I write down my life—and more and more I feel impelled to do so—he will represent a central figure.

And so they who understood him most profoundly frustrate the wish that gave his life meaning and integrity; his closest friends are dragging him back into daylight. It is impossible for any of them to do otherwise: so imbued with him are they that it would be hypocrisy for them not to talk about him.

It grieves me that I cannot tell him why it is impossible for me not to talk about him. I could tell him in a way that he would understand, and then I could count on his forgiveness, which he would not even speak out loud.

It is from Sonne, that most detailed and articulate of speakers, that I learned what silence is. He alone has given me that longing for silence, and if it is unattainable for me and will always be so—even in death I will be incapable of silence—still, I know, thanks to him, what it is: the best.

I wonder whether Sonne could be silent even in paradise.

He never writes the works he has announced, so that he can write things no one expects.

On days like this, to step ecstatically into the light as often as possible. To run into every dark corner, just to step back joyfully into the light, ecstatically.

What is it, this love for the resonant names of old gods? Is it not finally just the pride in our own expanding self, which has created room enough for them? Does it replace the languages we never learned, since it is so much easier to content ourselves with names of gods? Or is it more? Is it our atonement for the monotheism our ancestors imposed on the world, the impoverishment and desolation that they brought down upon us with it?

I feel guilty about the power with which the Bible still often overcomes me; the guilt never stops, and it has been with me since early youth.

The reflected glory of yesterday! Water, speaking.

It might be possible to show how a person could be *created* from praise. You would have to quote those words of praise that penetrated early on and leave the rest out. The result would be the fearful body of praise that finally made up that person.

Some words of praise become as essential as air and food. What a person won't do to get them back, when the usual source has closed down, when no more praise is coming. Make up some crazy thing consisting of praise alone. Devise a method of making praise ineffective by neutralizing it on the spot with an antidote.

Someone who has never been praised. What does he look like? How does he move? How does he live?

Someone who knows how to vomit forth praise.

One who bathes in puddles of praise and comes out dirty.

One who, rodentlike, stores praise in his cheeks.

One who poisons all around him with praise.

One who is sensitive only to collective praise, not even noticing what individuals say.

A praise preserver.

A praise digester.

A praise transformer: everything he hears becomes a single word that he hears and hears till his eardrums burst, and then he still hears it through his skin and nose.

A club of epicures, exchanging praise.

One who wastes away, ashamed of praise, and dies.

One who knows that all praise is false and who doesn't really expect any more. But he can't quite keep from listening for it.

One who is transformed by praise, becoming this or that, in turn, but is nothing without being sparked by praise.

One who, for praise, puts on his best suit.

One who has stopped doing everything, so as not to miss a word of praise. In the end he dares not even open his mouth, for fear he will not hear some praising word, and dies of hunger.

He now only says what has been said about him. His memory failing, he reads from notes.

One who classifies friends by how well they praise him.

One who needs people who praise others as well.

One who allows praise only via telephone, so as not to be distracted by anything else.

One who steals others' telegrams of praise.

One who wants only the praise appropriate for others.

One who puts on weight with praise.

One who believes praise only if it means money.

One who so hates praise that everyone who wants something from him approaches him with words of reproach.

One who defaces every picture of himself.

A woman who can only give praise while being loved.

One who believes in God only while being praised.

One who hates praise violently because others, too, get praise.

Sufficient praise, but not nearly enough to continue.

Hearing false statements, he positively blossoms; he knows everything so much better!

What I have brought back with me from this trip: Pessoa.

How can I believe that I was Pessoa's contemporary for thirty years?

Basically I never wanted to do anything more than to splinter myself, like Pessoa, into a small number of figures, which I steadfastly retain.

Everything we record is already too old.

I come alive when I narrate orally. It doesn't matter to whom—it just has to be spontaneous and without pre-conditions. I can't know in advance what I will say. It cannot be repeated and it has to take me by surprise.

So I depend on ears and am unutterably thankful to those who have ears for me. But they cannot be idle ears, they can't fake anything, and I have to get the feeling that I could keep them open a thousand days and nights.

It is always painful for me when I stop narrating. It is this pain that keeps me alive.

G. is his mother's victim. He ascribes his having outlived her by thirty-three years to a trick of his psyche: he con-tinues to live as he would have with her and has excluded every other woman from his life. The disease she died of has become his calling and his science, and both remain a strenuous attempt to cure her. A gentle, tender man, he has sacrificed thousands of guinea pigs for her. But she never has, never will have, enough. The real victim he sees in her, not in himself. Even now he would freely give up his life to save hers. In these thirty-three years there has always been something physically wrong with him, to keep the wound of separation from her fresh. In his mind she seems as alive today as then. If anyone has ever been a slave of love, it is he. When he can, he brings home a new token of veneration in memory of her. He knows how untamable are the demands of her ambition, and he bears it, too, beneath his abraded skin.

He sometimes gets lost in his library. He snatches one wrong book after another and reads, his anger growing. He gets worked up, then he grabs the next one. He knows nothing will come of this pursuit. He only wants to get worked up.

He grabbed the nosy snoop by the snout and tied him— it—up.

Before his death a man distributes his wealth to people whom he likes at first sight. He walks the street looking for them. The moment he likes someone, he immediately gives that person what anyone else would only bequeath. This activity, which makes him happy, takes him a long time. He drags it out and gives away less and less. He needs a lot of tact to avoid antagonizing people. Women believe him right away, though some are disappointed that he doesn't expect anything from them for the money. But by and large his candidates soon disappear, for fear he might change his mind.

Should chance bring him back to the same region, no one will admit knowing him.

"And that the likes of Shelley, Hölderlin, and Leopardi perish in misery means nothing; I think very little of such men."

Friedrich Nietzsche

"May the God to whom I prayed as a child forgive me! I cannot understand Death in his world."
Friedrich Hölderlin to Friedrich Neuffer. Letter from Jena, *May 8, 1795*

The Jews' obedience to God, that which has preserved them over the centuries, irritates me. In their wisest, most wonderful stories, there is always this obedience. How I love their *readers*, who remain poor because they read but who are nonetheless accorded the highest respect! How I love the sense of justice Jews demand of people, their patience, often their kindness! But their obedience to the never-ending threat of God disgusts me. I know in this I am a child of my time. I have been a witness to too much obedience. And one need hardly still say it: those against God were the most obedient, but their obedience was a model and the brutes would settle for nothing less. The constant bowing I saw as a child was repeated for the visible rulers of the world to horrific effect.

Can we stand up against a visible lord if we have no invisible lord? A trying question.

There have never been greater barbarians than we. We must look for our humanity in the past. (Objection to *Crowds and Power*.)

I wish to know much, thus I have respect for science. But I shall never be its slave, just as in a former age I would never have been a slave of theology.

Erna P. was in Venice when Schnitzler's daughter committed suicide. She knew the young Italian officer with whom the daughter had fallen in love. She had been present when the two met in Saint Mark's Square. The young man wore his Fascist uniform with conviction. Schnitzler was horrified by his daughter's decision to marry the man. He was emphatically against it. His wife, Olga, who was in Venice and knew the good-looking Italian, wrote him that he should remember certain things he had written. Schnitzler's answer: "Don't quote my own works to me." The marriage came about and ended soon after with his daughter's suicide. In Venice it was rumored that she had caught her mother and her husband in flagrante. Erna thought this story was so well-founded that no one who knew the people involved would have doubted the truth of it.

(Erna has much to tell about the people she knew; they included some very interesting characters. When talking about private matters that occurred forty years ago, she speaks very haltingly and softly, as if she were committing a great indiscretion. She implies that the things she is telling me she has never told another soul. She regards them as confidences and almost adds, "No one must ever hear this."

She has forgotten nothing, is very accurate, and, one can be certain, never exaggerates. She is speaking not as a painter but as a zoologist.)

The missing heart of things: their noncreatedness.

"The Earl of Portsmouth would slaughter his own cattle with an axe, shouting, 'That serves them right! The ambitious toads!' "

A man arrives who has counted his hair. He counts it daily. It's not thinning—but he must not lose a single strand. His job is to be sure that he always has the same number of hairs. He does his job well and prides himself on it. You just have to see him make his entrance, a clear conscience on his sleeve and a withering glance at all the people whose hair isn't counted. "How nice the world would be if everyone counted their hair. There would be no discontent, because there would be no disorder."

He is convinced that disorder is irrevocably linked with one's hair. He knows people who would not be nearly so bad, if only they had enough character to realize this. So he looks everyone he runs into straight in the eye and estimates the number of hairs they have. Of course, the job isn't really done with just an estimate, but it's better than nothing.

It is part of his task to keep quiet. The reason for his contentment is his secret. But he keeps his head high and counts his "population" every day. It is not an easy job, for he has a lot of hair. He has nimble fingers. How does he do it? To know that, you'd have to count hair every day.

1971

He is offended that he cannot get even the stupidest man on earth to listen to him.

His hoary, hairy, overgrown wisdom. To reacquire it would take him three lifetimes. Only what he knew at fifteen remains as alive as it was then. Everything more recent is dormant and that which is most recent is in the deepest sleep.

He only hears you when he has *smelled* you.

A little more concision, and I can say I am writing Chinese.

I most mistrust the moral rules with which I am obsessed.
   But nothing seems more contemptible to me than simply throwing them overboard, as N. did.
   I certainly have something to say about the awful enlargement of the ego. But I also know that it means *noth-*

ing, that it is a wretched self-deception about death, against which it is no help at all.

When he is around books, he can't get drunk; they are their own kind of wine.

Every truth irritates me that I have not discovered this very moment, in a flash.

Pi-chi. Brush sketches of the Sung dynasty.
Pi-chi (miscellaneous notes). These consist of short notes of the most various sort, on literature, art, politics, archaeology, all mixed together. The pi-chi are a treasure house for the history of the culture of the time; they contain many details, often of importance, about China's neighboring peoples.
They were intended to serve as suggestions for learned conversation when scholars came together; they aimed at showing how wide was a scholar's knowledge.

Wolfram Eberhard

So, without realizing it, I have rediscovered in my sketches an ancient Chinese form. It is not arrogance or vain fancy that despite my ignorance of the language I love everything Chinese.
It would be good to research the extent to which the Japanese pillow books were inspired by pi-chi (it would have been possible historically). Long ago, in Vienna, I

stumbled on the pillow book of Sei Shonagon, and I have read countless times the excerpts from it available to me.

"Bunin could hardly keep pace with the old man, who had started running and kept repeating in a wild, broken tone of voice, 'There is no death! There is no death!' " (On Tolstoy)

It could well be that one day I will *submit* and die. I beg all who may hear of it for forgiveness.

I am reminded of much in my own life, since reading Tolstoy's. Life is infectious, and remembrance no less so.

I sense a great desire to write my life down, not all of it, of course, but certain parts. I am very much afraid that I will not get to it and that it will all be lost, which would be a great pity.

It wouldn't matter where I started. There would be a lot to say about every phase.

I used to say that it was a kind of resignation to write one's life down, as if one had no plans to do anything further. It never occurred to me that there are writers who *began* their careers with the depiction of their youth and who nevertheless afterward wrote one work after another. This not-so-rare event never occurred to me until now, as I am reading Tolstoy, and it hit me like a bolt from the blue.

Someday I want to find out what I really *revere*. I want to bring together the figures from every area that I still revere today.

One never thinks of them together. They are very scattered, some of them at times forgotten.

I don't think I am harming them by bringing them together once. It need not just annoy them; they might actually find it *amusing*.

We accord ourselves the reverence we withhold from others. So the inability to revere others is questionable.

I could never have guessed that the moon landing would be capable of destroying *the* religion of my life that seemed the most secure. There is no indestructible religion; what happened to this one is—given its vivid presentation— simply more apparent.

". . . that nothing that is his own could ever impress a man." (A useful aperçu from Gombrowicz's diaries.)

Do *not* avoid the word "story" (in the sense of an account). But *do* avoid "text."

He particularly loves those he will never see again.

She only sees what is behind the scenes. Beyond that she sees nothing.

Appetite goes in circles there, and one person eats after the next.

What makes Buddhism so colorful?

Its extension over such a wide area? The variety of people who have absorbed it?

Why is Christianity so much less colorful?

Because its seats of power have been so well known to us for so long? Or because it so rarely includes animals and treats them so trivially?

This last reason has much to recommend it. Everything having to do with Saint Francis is exciting. Once I stopped in my tracks before a painting by Veronese in the Galleria Borghese, *Saint Anthony Preaching to the Fishes*, as if it were a miracle. No Madonna could ever mean as much to me.

Christ on the cross *means* something when his pain is horrifying. But mostly he is just a pleasant, good-looking man. You could take him down from there and hear him talk as if nothing had happened. He makes death easier by making it seem pleasant.

The watering down of Christianity is unbearable to me when I think of the grandeur of the Sermon on the Mount or the agony of Christ's death.

If I lived in a Buddhist country, would I be aware of the watering down of Buddhism?

The decline cannot be quite the same, since Christianity is, at bottom, more intense and more violent. It includes killing, and Christ's suffering on the cross cannot be easy if it is to have any meaning.

In Buddhism, the founder's death is a gentle one, reached very slowly, through a spiritual process, not by external force. The exemplary aspect of these founding figures has always amazed me. I don't completely understand their effect even today.

Since their very existence necessarily excludes force, it could never degenerate into our particular kind of violence.

The colorfulness of Buddhism, which is where I began, derives, on the other hand, from the idea that gives it *eo ipso* its universality: the belief in the transmigration of souls.

Buddha once found his home in every existence. Compared with the Jataka, Buddha's nativity stories, the hagiographies of the Church seem rather monotone.

The existence of Buddha, who once was *all*, is the fullest existence attributed to any creature in history. At its core this religion has remained colorful no matter how much it may have paled or degenerated in practice.

On his birthday, Swift would read the Book of Job.

That we can no longer escape history is for me the most depressing idea of all.

Is this the real reason I bother with myths? Am I hoping to find a forgotten myth that might save us from history?

The Carper. Abul Khattib is proclaiming God. Sitting here amidst the rest of us confused scions of the West, he wails a hundred times a day, "The East! The East!"

Though opposed to sagacity, he knows all. He writes stories in Urdu and has them translated as cheaply as possible. The young gather round him—Germans, English, Swiss, French—and he carpingly rattles off what each of their countries lacks. They listen respectfully, some because they have a private longing for moralistic speeches, others because they don't want him to feel that his skin is brown. He is treated with kid gloves and likes it here. He would like to publish his stories in every country there is, and when he is looking for publishers, he smiles sweetly. So he is not always carping—he can flatter when he wants something.

But he is really only himself when he is carping on the spiritual values of the East. One wonders what he would do if there were no East and West. He would have to switch to North and South.

It is useless to ask him about the last election results in Pakistan. He has less to say about those than what you can read in the papers. The little he knows he speaks as if it were a revelation. He lives here as a journalist and writes for newspapers in Pakistan and India. That's what he says, and you have to believe him, he rails so against lies. But when he talks about his homeland, he knows more than he tells. He conceals everything that might denigrate the "East."

Often, when he speaks of the grinding poverty of his homeland, his harangues grow incoherent. Then you even suspect empathy behind the words. They always sound like an accusation of the wealthy West. Since you know how right he is, you feel guilty. You feel guilty because you live here and you are much too well-off. But he quickly leaves these materialistic depths and jumps over to God and spiritual values. When he speaks of

"God," he carps the most. It's never clear whether he sees the plight of the East as resulting from the godlessness of the West or of the East itself. But after a few hours you decide on a simpler approach: he wants to attack those who do not have God, because he does have God. Aside from God there is nothing, he is capable of saying, and no misery beyond this can really affect him deeply. He sits in his corner quietly, like a spider—often covering sheets of paper with his language's beautiful script, flights of fancy in which he is unequaled—and waits for a victim. Barely does a young man who once heard him appear in the doorway than he smiles sweetly and greets him like an old friend, offering him a chair. He stops writing, and soon he can be plainly heard throughout the place, whining, "I hate nobody! I love every human being!" We try to ignore him, having heard him ten thousand times before, but the word "God" jumps out at us like a death threat and we freeze.

Suddenly the peoples of the world forgot what they were called. What happened?

His stories are sea swells, changing with the force and direction of the wind. He tells them a thousand times over, and they are never the same; when the air is calm he nearly forgets them. But then they become dark and angry and sweep away entire ships' crews.

To have a single idea for the first time and not know it.

People who can say only the opposite of what they believe in. To avoid causing displeasure they deny themselves to the point of death and think no one has noticed.

It bothers me that myths are called, bombastically, "myths" and fairy tales are called, childishly, "fairy tales."
 We should be brave enough to invent other names for these wonderful things.

He needs the discourse of narrowness as well, and what is dull drives him back into breadth.

He can only grasp certain fashionable ideas after he senses that they have been debunked and destroyed.

To get hold of a heart till it speaks: Dostoyevsky.

Confessions are too easy. It is impossible to see how man could become better.
 Laws were an early first attempt.
 They have proved themselves to the point that they have become a branch of knowledge.
 Undermined by our laws, nature puts more power in our hands than we can control.
 But the old laws end up in the hangman's hands.

All his life he sought a kind of freedom for mankind. But he always knew men were basically evil. What would these radically evil creatures do with their freedom? He is still for freedom, though. Because he knows what they are capable of under duress, he mistrusts that even more than freedom.

I like most to move within others and not be able to find my way out for a while.

You can only bear them by running away from them like a pawn and springing back again like a knight.

In the anarchic tangle of their hair they find freedom.

I have run about among all the gods. What a colorful life it's been! But too much fun—I didn't have to believe in them. So I had an easy time of it.

Now I need to be a little tougher on myself—but without Hegel.

Every report of the trip gets it more and more wrong. When you talk to someone about it, the experience is altered. Keeping quiet changes it too, differently.

There can be no report.

Other languages? Yes, but only to avoid our own, through clumsiness. After all, we need broken languages too.

The unrecognized friend: he stalks you to protect you.

Someone who escapes from the things of the world through their names.

An unexecutable order that takes an entire lifetime.

He goes crawling to her with seldom-used words. She misunderstands and yields to him.

There everyone can pick ten years to skip.

He lines up everyone he has persecuted with his hatred. The figure that results is himself.

She kept everything for herself until he gave it to her again.

The one fascinating thing about vengefulness is that it has a good memory. What it does is undignified. One takes revenge through kindness.

He has the dignity of a *thin* person, not reading himself into corpulence but picking pathways through the corpus of texts, taking care that these pathways constantly cross. But the junctions are new, and he is always reorienting himself.

He knows what matters at the moment, and this is mainly how he tries to guide himself. But he is sparing enough to be mindful of the past. He doesn't gorge on time; the past leaves no fat on him, only its mark.

All that it takes for him to avoid public places he visits too often is for him to talk with someone who might turn up again and continue the conversation.

He hates nothing more than a conversation's being continued. He prefers that every conversation occur once and once only.

A name has to have a *beginning*. Whatever you have done, no matter how wonderful, it means nothing to anyone before your name has *begun*. Once it has begun, it will keep growing faster and faster for less and less reason, for none at all. But how does a name begin?

In the past, it depended on chance, which no one could influence. Today we fabricate names on purpose, and the bearer of a name would have to be very dim indeed not to know how absolutely *meaningless* this artificial, mass-produced ornament really is.

The ordering of influences, dramatically demonstrated by the ordering of books. No sooner have influences been arranged than they fall asleep.

It is enough to submit to your thoughts for an hour a day, *pointlessly*, to stay somewhat human.

We are dangerously much and don't see all of ourselves. If we had complete insight into what we are, it would paralyze us and we would have to hold our breath till we fell down dead.

He doesn't know his own smell and hates it in others.

Eternity as a comet.

I can't praise correctly. I can't mete out gratitude properly. So much gets spilled along the way. It is better to add more right away.

I saw Alexandra Tolstoy, and she spoke about her father, about the night he fled, when he suddenly came to her and said, "I am going away forever."

Sixty-one years ago, and she talked about her sister Masha, who had died, and about her mother, who was crazy—she used the word *paranoia*—and about how her

(207)

mother lived nine years longer than he, found peace, and realized what she had done to him.

She spoke English when I saw her, dropping a Russian word now and then, as if to prove it was really she, Tolstoy's only daughter, his only living child.

Five years old when he died and still in Ruschuk, I heard his name from my mother in Vienna when I was ten. But only in the past few months, as I've been learning about his life, has he really become a part of me.

One who sucks all the poison out of books and administers it to those around him in careful doses.

This instinct he has for avoiding everything technical, deeming it knowledge and accomplishment. Not that he rejects the usual conveniences; he does make use of them, and they both ease and enliven his life. But he refuses to think about them; like a Greek, he grants them no status and treats them like slaves.

And thus he has remained open to all the puzzles that have ever been, breaking his teeth and bones on them.

The reason he is not impressed by riches is that he has never met anyone who was able to get rid of them quickly.

Sentences have not become exhausted. Not even close to it. Sentences are exhausted only for those who are compelled to break them to bits.

She watched him at prayer, and he prayed better.

"Give them limits, they need limits," he said, and turned the key in the lock and kept an eye fixed on him through the keyhole.

What did Adam do to God when he opened his eyes?

An enemy reveals himself to be the truest friend: reverse unmasking. Thus, there has to exist a counterdisease to paranoia. One does exist.

P. revolted me when he spoke of his spiritualist séances; he is convinced of an afterlife and wants to offer me these experiences and introduce me into his circle.

But to me, my dead are sacred; I don't wish to find them again in a circle of strangers.

To be more precise about the nature of *invention*: I think it always depends on your *starting point*. There do exist such things as the "germs" of invention; I know them and know they are irresistible. But I am not sure whether they differ from person to person or whether there is some kind of general supply of these "germs" that move all people everywhere to tell stories.

It is important to find belief, but in order to do so, we must ourselves believe what we have invented. We can know very well that we are making something up and yet believe it all the same. The sensation of expansion that we feel must be true, like another way of breathing, if we are to believe what we bring forth.

To be believable, the story must first of all arouse our astonishment: only the astounding will be believed. Anything obvious or everyday cannot be a story; since it doesn't arouse our astonishment, it is not believed.

All that matters is that we have a sense of what can astonish.

Part of this sense is excitement, the pure excitement of wonder. We see this clearly when children listen to fairy tales.

But it is odd that the same story can be told and retold and that despite its familiarity it can astonish us anew. We can tell it exactly the same way or totally differently. Variants are a concern of literature, and yet also something like impotence.

The reason for my aversion to "aesthetic" writers is their indulging themselves only in variants. Not only are they unable but they are unwilling to invent anything new. They must rely on what already exists or they don't believe even themselves.

And it's not just "refined" writers like Hofmannsthal that this applies to. There are "tougher" figures as well, like Brecht, who can't invent without considerable reliance on what already exists.

It seems that the immediate source of invention, the thing that sets it off, works differently for different people. Some people soon throw the original inspiration away, leaving everything behind in their headlong dash. Others make it a road that they stay right on, drifting off for no more than a centimeter or so before returning to it again. Brecht is one of those who stays true to his road. That is his charm, and he knows it. But he considers this limitation to be *more real* and mistrusts those who leave their original inspiration behind.

Invention is one of my most natural states of being, so it is time I tried to define precisely what is involved in it.

Nothing is more crippling for the inventive person than the presence of someone who is always asking, "And is it true?" The question arises out of the listener's closed world, which his fearfulness keeps him from leaving; he sticks to his own gut.

More than anything else, an inventor cannot abide people who are unable to forget their own guts. He avoids them like the plague.

The real creator gets bolder with age. He has more invention germs within him; in the course of his life they have multiplied. Of course, the danger for him is that he will be embarrassed to astonish or will be ashamed of showing his embarrassment. He is expected to know everything; nothing should be new for him or the general opinion of idiots will be that he hasn't experienced enough.

But the truth is that the more one has experienced, the more there is to be astonished by. Our capacity for wonder grows with experience, becomes more urgent.

How does the storyteller assure himself of the belief of his listeners? For one thing, by not giving them a moment's peace, burying them in an ever-growing heap of fabrications, into which he has apparently mixed the familiar. These quiet places are the springboards from which he propels himself off again. In his torrent of invention they have to be very easy to spot and incredibly simple, so one can push oneself off from them again.

Some inventive people wait too long and so have the effect of appearing too reasonable. As soon as we don't expect anything from them, we don't believe them either. One other thing: the inventor mustn't stay in the foreground. He himself is unimportant; we don't want to know anything about him personally. The only interesting thing about him is the process of invention itself: one could easily imagine a man's inventing things, day after day, night after night, for years and decades, without knowing the least thing about himself.

He wants to know more than what is contained in books. But he wants to know everything that's in them as well.

A writer who doesn't have a wound that's always open is no writer for me. He may prefer to hide it if (out of pride) he doesn't want pity, but he must have one.

Future-sick: he cannot bear the thought of the future, not of a specific future—a particularly bad one, say—but of every future.

A green window in the distance and in it, once a year, a light.

I have tracked down every childhood memory of anything involving masses; I have distorted nothing. But I have lost my earliest memory of *leaves*.

It is impossible to keep silent when someone dies. We demand a howling pack to grieve with us, and when none is available, we look to find one by sending off letters.

But the power of our grief is so great that we do not write just to people who knew the dead person, we force everyone we know to honor the memory of that person. We introduce our dead to them retroactively, summoning the best that we can say about them. We make it very plain how much the person meant to us, applying a kind of pressure on our friends: woe to him who does not feel the same way. We secretly make the continuation of our friendship with them dependent on how they react to the death notice. We test them, watch them suspiciously. We weigh every word of their reaction carefully in the balance; if it is too light, we reject it mercilessly, and they will never be part of us again.

I find it difficult to *learn* any more; something compels me to react to everything immediately. I can no longer retain anything without being touched by it.

He has one eye in back and one in front and sees the same with either one. (The mistrustful one.)

To rediscover all those useless words and drown in them for shame.

He laughs with his liver, I laugh with my ear.

Obsessed with Nothing, he is constantly putting things in order. Without order, he could not bear Nothing. In a Nothing that's orderly he feels cozy.

Perched there, a spider in his web of order, he need not ask himself what will happen.

For all that could happen would be Nothing, and he has that under control.

A smile whose innocence lies in its intelligence. It recognizes and approves what it observes. Without arrogance, it knows it to be its own.

Exhausted by decisions. Invigorated by decisions.

Observe the other, not always the self.

Montaigne, the visitor, is stabbed by Torquato Tasso gone mad.

God seeks a man who has never heard his name and bows down in gratitude before a deaf and dumb beggar.

Eight men, old as the hills, living off a coin that no one knows.

Swift treads on Quevedo's heels and makes no apology.

The man who was duped makes up the stories that led to his duping and savors them.

He refuses to speak to people he knows. He speaks only to strangers.

A sign of respect: to pass by someone more quickly.
Confucius, Conversations

Creel at the end of his book on Confucius: "He trusted the human race." A very beautiful thought.

We learn the wisdom of foreign cultures to gain perspective on our own. Whatever familiarity has made meaningless or dubious suddenly gains new life through distance. We must see this from afar, without warning. We don't know when we will see it again; we don't realize it is what we are after. It appears all of a sudden, like something we forgot in our preoccupation with the exotic, like an unexpected and surprising view.

And so we have to recollect all that which was as close to us as our own skin.

Basically I don't trust anyone who calls himself a poet, especially not the self-styled poet who really *is* one.

For he would know it all depends on words alone, and not on him. What more can he do with words, astounding and uncanny as they are even before his involvement with them? What is his little juggling act weighed against the splendor of words as they are, as he found them, as they remain! He should be grateful that they allow him to handle them. He should be ashamed he has never appreciated them. He should think of those who have appreciated them better. He should be mindful of those who should never handle them.

All that remains of past generations is contained in words handed down. This treasure is so huge that no single person can absorb or contain it within himself. The little bit of philosophy we pride ourselves on consists of attempts to take seriously some few of these words at the expense of all the rest.

François Villon as a censor of modern lyrics, and how he corrects them.

We can talk only about the same things, over and over. Fine, if they're not too few.

A woman who remembers every man who got away but who has forgotten all those who loved her.

Surrounded by angels he alone saw, he traveled through the world, observing them in silence. He never drew attention to himself, never said a thing. If he missed anything, the angels would warn him until he saw it himself.

Fufluns, the Etruscan god of delight.

In the play of language, death disappears.

He distills his blood with music. His twelve-room house a retort.

How much hate does it take to destroy the world? When will it start to defend itself?

"The Muisca believed an ordinary man could not bear to look upon the prince with impunity. For this reason it was the custom to sentence criminals to gaze now and then at the prince."

He gave the moon for the blue of a peacock's throat and landed on that patch of peacock blue.

The Battle of the Short Words and the Long Words by Brueghel.

The smiling mummy with hair three meters long. He saw her, bought her, and brought her home. She hangs before him now, a thousand years old, two thousand? Teeth, in her crooked mouth, are a mockery. Her chin barely resting on her narrow, delicate hand. What does she wish for, since being dug up in the New World? Even as she was first decomposing, her world was not new. And did she have as many admirers back then? Was her hair already this long, or has it grown only for us?

Today I saw G. on the railway platform in Grenoble. I was in the moving train and he was standing there waving, getting smaller and smaller. It was him, I recognized him. Is it a miracle that he, who loved movies so much, had slipped into one himself? And in Grenoble, where I had come to visit him?